James Payn

At her Mercy

Vol. 1

James Payn

At her Mercy
Vol. 1

ISBN/EAN: 9783337346447

Printed in Europe, USA, Canada, Australia, Japan

Cover: Foto ©Thomas Meinert / pixelio.de

More available books at **www.hansebooks.com**

A Novel.

BY THE AUTHOR OF
"LOST SIR MASSINGBERD,"
ETC., ETC.

IN THREE VOLUMES.
VOL. I.

LONDON:
RICHARD BENTLEY AND SON.
1874.
(All Rights Reserved.)

THIS BOOK

IS

Affectionately Dedicated

TO

WILLIAM JAMES EDLIN.

CONTENTS OF VOL. I.

CHAPTER	PAGE
I. "A MEDICAL OPINION"	1
II. WHAT DUNWICH THOUGHT ABOUT IT	25
III. A DUEL BETWEEN PRINCIPLES	39
IV. A LOVING FAREWELL	58
V. IN WHICH LORD DIRLETON OVERREACHES HIMSELF	79
VI. BALCOMBE	102
VII. A NEW PROFESSION	116
VIII. IN WHICH MR. ANGELO HULET IS "UPSET"	137
IX. IN THE LADIES' DRAWING-ROOM	151
X. JUDITH'S LITTLE SUGGESTION	173
XI. THE RING AND THE RING GUARD	203
XII. UNDER THE GREENWOOD TREE	223
XIII. EVY ASKS A FAVOUR	240
XIV. AN UNWILLING CONFIDENCE	256
XV. CLIFF COTTAGE	274

AT HER MERCY.

CHAPTER I.

"A MEDICAL OPINION."

IN the heart of England lies Dunwich, loveliest village, not of the plain, but of the hill top. You must climb up from the rich levels where the hop gardens lie, through half a mile of hanging wood—nature's own refrigerator—ere you arrive on an August morning such as this, refreshed and cool, in that "haunt of ancient peace" and (what, alas, is more rare) of plenty. For there are no poor at Dunwich—absolutely none. Small as the place is, it contains two venerable almshouses which absorb the aged and infirm, who having done their life's work, or failed in doing it (God alone knows why), fold their wrinkled palms, awaiting the Divine summons, and whom we call our surplus population. These dwellings have no affinity to the almshouse of the nation—the workhouse. Except that they are one-storied, they resemble colleges, each with its green court within it, like a huge emerald in a fair stone setting; the gray walls are overgrown with moss and lichen; even the ivy is cut away with no remorseless hand, for all things that are old, or have an attachment to what is old, are here held sacred. In Seymour's Home, the smaller of the two, the doors have gray stone porches, in which the inmates sit on summer eves, and knit or read, or, since the building commands the valley, look down upon the happy autumn fields, and think, or not think (probably only doze and dream), on the days that are no more; a thoughtful spectacle enough to others at all events.

Every dwelling on the south and north of straggling Dunwich Street, commands a lovely prospect; and the houses are happily not contiguous, so that between the gaps, the wayfarer has glimpses of both landscapes, the one, at this time, shining with the gold of harvest, and the green of the hop-crops, the other waving with woodlands as far as eye can reach. Even the windows that give upon the street have a fair outlook, and not only through these gaps aforesaid, for before every house is more or less of garden, and in almost every garden is a tree. It seems as though instead of desolating a village to make a hunting ground, as his fellows too often did, that the feudal lord of Dunwich had permitted the village to be built in his own leafy demesne, with the sole proviso that his trees should be spared.

The great gates of the modern park (it was once a chase) stand close to Seymour's Home, in the very centre of the hamlet, and are open night and day to all comers. Thus without descending from their high-placed Paradise, the happy Dunwich folks can pass from their own doors into a world of verdurous "dip," and upland, with groves of stately oak, and dells of fern, where the couched deer, accustomed to such harmless visitors, scarce lift their branching heads to watch them pass. Here and there, beneath some spreading tree, or on some hillock whence the leafy avenue prolongs itself to one green arbour, and seems to meet at last, are rustic seats "for whispering lovers made," or at all events such intention is taken for granted, and they are used accordingly. In place of high blank walls, which the baser Rich too often build about their beauteous homes to bar their fellows' eyes from all fruition of them, and bolted gates with cold uncivil menials to reflect their master's harshness, the lord of Dunwich permits all to share his woodland treasures; nay, better than those "great sirs," who,

> " Give up their parks a dozen times a year,
> To let the people breathe,"

he welcomes them the whole year through, as though he held his lands in fee of them. On the whole, then, with their common park, and their fair prospects from their doors, and their almshouses to retire into, if the worst came to the worst with them, one might well suppose that the inhabitants of Dunwich had little cause for complaint; yet, if so, one would be very much mistaken. With Mr. Angelo Hulet, for instance, a bachelor or widower (it was not quite understood which) of some substance, who had been settled in the village these ten years, and had, therefore, some right, he imagined, to speak with authority upon the subject, this very openness of the park was a grievance.

"I call it a deuced impertinent thing," he would argue, "of my Lord Dirleton, or of any other lord, to offer his patronage in this sort of way. It is only an underhand way of making slaves of the people. He first lays them under an obligation, and then expects to see them on their knees before him; but he will never catch Angelo Hulet in that position."

Why "Angelo," none but this independent gentleman's godfathers and godmothers (long since dead) could have explained, if even they; but, as to the "Hulet," he had a great deal of information to offer. In his little study, as he calls it, a charming apartment opening on a smoothed-shaved lawn, from which three fair counties are visible, as you sit under the tall cedar in its centre (from which the house derives its name, the Cedars), there hangs a picture, whereby hangs a tale. It is the representation of a man in a vizor, with a long gray beard, who leans on a headsman's axe. He is standing on a scaffold with the block beside him, and beneath it there is a great crowd of people, chiefly soldiers; and this scaffold is, so to speak, the proprietor of the picture's "platform," whereupon he dilates to an impatient and unsympathizing world upon the death of that perfidious monarch Charles the First, whose head was cut off by William, sergeant in Colonel Hewson's regiment, and founder of the race of Hulet.

It is not to be supposed, however, that the present descendant of that hero inherits in any way his truculent character. Mr. Angelo Hulet is the mildest-mannered man that ever scuttled ship of the state in traitorous speech; a hypochondriac and a valetudinarian. His study contains a bookcase stored, not with republican works, but with all the classical literature upon Indigestion; and beneath the book-case is a cupboard, filled with every sovereign cure for the nerves, from "digestive tablets" to prussic acid. At the time of our introduction to him he is a little over sixty years of age, but presents the appearance, possibly from too free an indulgence in those excellent remedies, of a man of seventy. He is tall and spare, with a slight stoop. His face is handsome but deeply lined, and, to a disciple of Lavater, the resolute fixity of jaw contrasts itself curiously with the indecisive expression of the eyes. These are never still, and when you speak to him, instead of concentrating themselves upon your own eyes, they shift and wander as though to escape their gaze. To judge him as dishonest, and afraid to look you in the face, on account of this peculiarity, would be, however, to do him a great injustice; it is only a nervous habit, which he uses with a stranger neither more nor less than with Evy his niece, and the ruler of his comfortable little household.

Eva Carthew had lost both her parents in a single day. They were on their way from India, chiefly to see the daughter they had sent to England quite a child, and of whom they had heard such glowing accounts from time to time from the schoolmistress to whom they had confided her, as made their hearts to leap for joy, when, within two days' sail of home, their vessel foundered. Eva's father had been an officer of rank, and in the enjoyment of a good income; but with him it died, and it would have gone hard with the orphan girl, then but just fifteen, had not Uncle Angelo held out his helpful hand to her. It had never been offered to her before, nor even had she so much as seen him,

Colonel Carthew and his brother-in-law had not been on good terms; indeed, they had despised one another very heartily, a state of things which had had its origin nearly two hundred years ago, for it arose out of that very "Chop at the King's Head," as Angelo irreverently termed it, or "the murder of our most gracious sovereign Charles the First," as the colonel designated that much-debated historical catastrophe. The hatchet that they could never bury was the one with which William Hulet slew his king. The subject had been always a bone of contention between them, and, on one occasion, the colonel, being his brother-in-law's guest, had so far forgotten that circumstance in the heat of controversy, as to rise and prick with a hot poker, not his host, indeed, but that which his host valued above himself, or professed to do so, the counterfeit presentment of his regicide ancestor. If you looked at the picture carefully, you might observe in the abdomen (for the assailant had no time to be particular) a large square patch, which had been let in to conceal the wound. Angelo Hulet never forgave that act of desecration; never spoke to his sister's husband nor his sister afterwards; and hated the innocent cause of that estrangement, Charles the First, more cordially than before. If, however, his heart had not yearned to go and see his little niece, exiled from her parents, and passing even her holidays under the roof of her schoolmistress, it had often reproached him with his neglect; "if Eleanor had only written a line to ask him to go, or if that idiot, Carthew, had had the grace to apologise for his brutal violence"—but there came no letter till that sad one from the schoolmistress which told him that his enemy was gone whither Charles Stuart and William Hulet had gone before, to Heaven's judgment, and with him the sister with whom Angelo had been playmate, companion, counsellor (in all except her marriage; he had "never liked the man"), and the only one of his own blood (save one other) in the world. Then, to do him justice, Angelo Hulet put away from him all remembrance of the quarrel about the merits of that False Tyrant or Blessed Martyr, and leaving orders that the wound in the picture should be neatly healed (which he had hitherto kept open, like an issue, to keep his wrath alive and active, by constant contemplation of it), had set off forthwith for the genteel academy in Linden Grove, Battersea, where sorrowing Eva was, to lay his home and purse at her disposal.

He had found her, a lithe slender slip of a girl, with an abundance of rich brown hair, which, with her soft hazel eyes, had formed her chief charm at that time; but the promise of beauty had now ripened into full performance. At eighteen, Eva Carthew was the ornament of her uncle's home, the pride of his heart, and the acknowledged flower among the belles of Dunwich. Nor, though her beauty was of a dainty and even delicate sort, was she one of those hot-house plants of "the garden of girls," who shrink from the winds of Heaven, and pass their lives wrapped up as it were in cotton-wool. No matter for snow or rain, she rarely failed to take her daily walk, or at least to step across the street to Allen's Almshouse, and visit the ancient dames, to whom her coming was as a streak of sunshine in a waste of cold gray sky. Doctor Burne, the long-established medical authority of Dunwich, protested that she did more good in the village than all the drugs in his dispensary, and that without any "un-English mummery;" a contemptuous expression which was understood to comprehend, not only the institution, habit, and profession of Sisters of Mercy, but organized charity of all kinds; for the doctor was of the old school, and if he had had to paint an angel would have made her carry, instead of a palm branch, a bottle of port wine, and instead of a crown on her head, two half-crowns in her hand, to be given away where it seemed to be most wanted. But for Evy, it is doubtful whether the honest doctor could have kept on good terms with her Uncle Angelo, a man with whose opinions, and even with his numerous maladies (though their existence, real or supposed, was much to his own interest), he protested "he had hardly common patience."

His patience must have been a good deal tried, for every morning it was expected that he should present himself at the Cedars, feel Mr. Hulet's fluttering pulse, and examine his tongue (he used purposely to make him keep it out, ever so long: "There are novel symptoms here; some cymophanous pimples; we must look to this," &c., &c.) until his patient was half suffocated. When this professional interview was over, the doctor was wont to pay a complimentary visit to Evy in the drawing-room, as happened upon the particular morning we have in our mind.

"How are you, Doctor Burne? How is my uncle?"

"Excellent, my dear. I have persuaded him that he has a brand-new disease, unknown before to the human species, and he is consequently in the highest spirits."

"Oh, doctor, how can you? When you know, too, that he is really far from well."

"That is very true; but the state of his nerves is chiefly owing to his foolish apprehensions about them, and to the quarts of rubbishing stuff that he takes to cure them. Any means that succeed in making him give up those doses of prussic acid, for instance, of which he takes enough daily to poison the whole company of Dunwich Rifles, their captain included (how well that blush becomes you, Miss Evy!) are more than justifiable. If I can only persuade him to take my medicine instead, I will answer for it it will do him no harm."

"Nor good, I suppose you mean, you wicked impostor!"

"Bread pills, my dear; honest bread pills, with a little powder over them to smell nice and nasty, are what your uncle shall have." And the doctor rubbed his fat hands together, as though he were already concocting them, and chuckled till his red face grew purple.

"I am afraid he will only take all the other things as well," observed Evy, sighing.

"Perhaps; I told him, however, it would be dangerous—with all the gravity I could muster, and quoting the sentiments of a hanky-panky homœopathical book that I got hold of the other day—'It is highly unadvisable, sir,' said I, 'to continue simultaneously two courses of medicine, each of such considerable power.' And then, what do you think? I recommended him to take a brisk walk daily in the park. You know how he loves Dirleton Park." Here the jolly doctor fairly roared with laughter, and had to take out his pocket-handkerchief to dry his tears.

"Hush, hush; or my uncle will hear you. It is too bad of you to behave so to him; I don't like it, doctor."

"It's all for his good, my dear; it's all for his good," answered the old fellow, with something of serious apology in his tone, for he saw that his companion was really annoyed; "besides which, Miss Evy, I put in a word on your own account. When I said, 'you must take to walking in the park,' of course he flew into a deuce of a rage, and swore that he would see the park—— well, in a state of conflagration, first, and that he wouldn't then; to which I replied that of course he would please himself, but that there was nothing so wholesome as the smell of deer. ('Ah, but that's musk deer, isn't it?' said he, gravely—when I really thought I should have had a fit.) And then I attributed your own excellent health to the frequent walks that you took in Lord Dirleton's coverts. Now wasn't that a good stroke of business for you? and yet you were just now upon the point of being angry with me; you know you were."

"I wasn't angry, doctor; but I don't like to hear dear Uncle Angelo made such fun of. He has been very good to me, you know."

Her large hazel eyes grew liquid as she

spoke; not as the doctor's had done, however, but quite differently. The tears did not fall, but formed clear pools, in whose depths you could see, or at least her companion could, glistening infinitely fairer than any Sabrina, gratitude, love, pity.

"I beg your pardon, Miss Evy," said the doctor, who, though he was over-fond of banter, and had an unbecoming habit of wetting his thumb when he commenced to deal at whist, was in feeling a gentleman after a far higher pattern than the Chesterfield, once thought very well of, but now happily relegated to its proper place, the tailor's shop, "forgive me for forgetting to whom I spoke. There is no one better aware than myself that your uncle has a good heart, and that it is only his digestion which is out of order. Well, when I spoke of your health, it seems I was only just in time, for he told me that he had had it in his mind this very morning to stop your walking in the park altogether. There would have been a pretty kettle of fish! Why? Do you suppose, then, I don't know all about it—I, who am the walking repository of all the gossip of Dunwich! 'Why,' indeed! Is it possible that a being can be so young, so fair, and yet so desperately hypocritical! You positively beat your ancestor who hangs in the study yonder, my dear Miss Evy, when he dropped a tear upon his regicidal axe, and begged the king's pardon before cutting his head off. Of course I know all about it— the walks in the greenwood glade, and the talks on the seat beneath the chestnut—so that when your uncle put this question categorically, 'Are you certain that the air in the park does her any particular good?' I replied, most honestly, 'The heir of that park is essential to her.' A doctor, fortunately for you, does not write out his opinion, or else he must needs have discovered at once that I meant Captain Heyton."

"Captain Heyton is not Lord Dirleton's heir—at least, not necessarily so," observed Evy, coldly.

She had blushed and trembled at first, like a rose when the warm south wind blows, at the doctor's too significant raillery; but she was calmly contemptuous of it by this time, and after the manner of her sex, had seized upon his last words to make a diversion in the embarrassing topic.

"He is the heir-presumptive, however, you little prevaricatrix," answered the other; "and presumption (especially where there is a great deal of it, as in his case) goes a great way. The idea of his standing yonder at this moment under the porch of Dame Swithin's cottage without the excuse of a drop of rain, and staring up at the Cedars—no, no, he is not there (for Evy's love-lit eyes had been unable to resist a furtive glance out of the window); but the idea of his doing so (I was about to observe) would not surprise me. There, I am a nasty disagreeable old teaze, you are thinking, perhaps; but the fact is, dear Miss Evy, I had a reason for my cruel conduct; I wanted to make myself quite sure, for your own sake, of how matters stood between you and the captain. I had never seen him when walking with a fair companion in the Home Wood press her willing hand, or heard him murmur like a dove —a ring-dove—that there was 'none like her, none,' though the presumption was that he had done it; but now that you have confessed as much—nay, pardon me, you have—I know how to proceed in your interests. Your uncle is thinking of leaving Dunwich."

"Leaving Dunwich!" echoed Evy, with a piteous stress on the name of the beloved village where she had known nought but happiness, and which for the last three months had been Paradise itself (for the doctor's diagnosis had been correct.) "What reason can he have for doing that?"

"Well, not a very strong one, my dear, in one sense—it's his nerves. He has heard from somebody that Balcombe—a place on the southern sea-coast somewhere —is good for his complaint; I mean his old one; and that is why I found out a new one for him this morning, to which Balcombe air will be very disadvantageous— that is, if you choose it so to be. He is to have my opinion to-morrow, when I shall have thought the matter over. Of course I want you to stop here; but I would not have humbugged your uncle on my own account; my principles are too strong for that; whereas for your sake I am prepared to enter upon a career of unblushing deceit. *Now* am I a cruel old inquisitor? *Now* am I a hard-hearted wretch, eh?"

"Indeed, doctor, I know you have the kindest heart in the world——"

"Softest you mean; soft as fresh butter, with your sweet image imprinted on it. (She has given me medicines to make me love her; it is certain she has given me medicines.) Well, go on."

"I was going to say, doctor, that if you are quite sure that Balcombe would do dear uncle no good, I would very much rather we did not leave Dunwich."

"Very good, my dear. Then if my medical dictum can decide the affair in Dunwich you shall stop—— But, I say, do look out of window. It is not an idea this time, for such a thing would never have entered into my head. No other man in the parish treads so gingerly over the stones as that. It is he himself—Lord Dirleton is coming across the street, and, if I am not mistaken, to the door of this very house; and that's his ring."

CHAPTER II.

WHAT DUNWICH THOUGHT ABOUT IT.

IT must not be supposed from the interview between Dr. Burne and Eva, that the latter was of a disposition underhand, or even unduly reticent. She loved her uncle well, but he was not one to invite any one's confidence, and certainly not the tender confession of a girl's first love. Upon his own affairs he kept an unbroken silence. Of his former life his niece knew absolutely nothing, save what, as a child, she had learnt from her mother's lips; that he had once been married, and that his marriage had turned out "unfortunately." As she grew up, the term had found a meaning for her that had hushed all questioning. Whatever had been the nature of his matrimonial catastrophe, it had, without doubt, rendered him very hostile to the married state, and prone to jest with bitter cynicism at love and lovers. Upon the whole, then, it was not surprising that Evy had kept her affection for Captain Heyton a secret from her uncle, and, as she had vainly hoped, from all the world.

As a matter of fact, there was nobody in Dunwich, except Mr. Angelo Hulet, who was not aware that there was "something between" his pretty niece and the gallant captain, though opinions were much divided upon its nature. Most people thought it was only a flirtation, and those who did not, with a few exceptions, pretended to think so. The five Miss Colvilles of the Grange, who held a highly respectable county position, and might themselves have made alliance with the noble house of Dirleton without "incongruity" (that was the term), affected to pity "that poor girl," Miss Carthew, with whom John Heyton was "making himself so ridiculous." Lady Wapshaw on the other hand (widow of Sir Richard Wapshaw, late Alderman of London), of Dunwich Castle, a very modern mansion, with an architectural salt-box at either wing, and an architectural watch-pocket with turrets in the centre—and who possessed one rather pretty and very marriageable daughter—protested that Evy would "deserve whatever she got," that is, she was understood to imply, provided it was something of a disappointing nature. She had no patience with young women who threw themselves at the heads of young men in a superior station of life to themselves, and for her part, thanked Heaven that Captain Heyton had never met the girl under her roof. Even Mrs. Mellish, the rector's wife, with whom Eva was a great favourite, was compelled to admit, under the influence of these great authorities, that " the whole affair was to be regretted," though she positively declined to accept the position they would have forced on her of volunteer Mentor, and adviser "for her good," to the young lady in question.

" It is your bounden duty as wife of the clergyman of the parish," urged Lady Wapshaw, " to depict to this motherless girl the abyss upon which she stands."

"Without going so far as that," said Mrs. Colville, " I think a word in season from you—or, perhaps, some little convincing tract upon ambition—might be of the greatest service. Or could you not get your husband to point seriously out to her that she has set her heart upon a Dead Sea apple, with nothing inside of it."

"Oh, as to that," interposed the titled

lady, contemptuously, " she would jump at it all the same. What does she care whether Captain Heyton is clever or stupid."

" I was speaking rather in a metaphorical sense," explained Mrs. Colville. " I think the unreasonableness of her pretensions should be dwelt upon—her uncle coming as he does from nobody knows where——"

" And going to a place about which there can be no possible doubt," put in Lady Wapshaw, acidly. " A man who walks out of church because he won't listen to the service about Charles the First, and kicks over the basket of oak-apples that is brought to his house on the 29th of May—"

" And of whom so little is known that it is doubtful whether he is a bachelor or a widower," continued Mrs. Colville. " Think of the gulf—the social gulf—between such a man and Lord Dirleton."

Good-natured little Mrs. Mellish looked

nervously from one to the other, like a bright-eyed bird in a cage between two cats. "It's very unfortunate, certainly," she murmured, "and much to be deplored."

"Pray say it's 'injudicious,'" sneered Lady Wapshaw, "as you said of those wretches who poached in the Home Wood under his lordship's nose."

"Indeed, madam," replied Mrs. Mellish, with some dignity, "I cannot honestly say much worse of it. Eva Carthew is a very sweet girl, and the daughter of an officer of distinction. Of course it would be a great advancement to her—perhaps an unwise advancement——"

"You are surely not supposing a marriage, my dear Mrs. Mellish?" interrupted Lady Wapshaw.

"I am certainly not supposing anything less than marriage," returned the little woman, her bright eyes glancing scorn, her feathers ruffled to their very quills. "And in this house you must give me leave to say, that I will not have anything less suggested. You don't know Evy Carthew as I know her. She is as simple as a—dear me," said Mrs. Mellish, looking about for a metaphor, for flights of eloquence were very unusual with her, "think of the very simplest of God's creatures——"

"Such as the fox," muttered Lady Wapshaw, fortunately beneath her breath.

"I honestly believe," continued Mrs. Mellish, eagerly, "that if that dear girl has fallen in love with Captain Heyton (mind, I don't say she has or she hasn't), that she loves him for his own sake, and without a thought of his brilliant expectations."

"And I honestly believe," said Lady Wapshaw, rising from her seat, with a contemptuous smile, "that if the present Lord Dirleton, in his sixtieth autumn and his twentieth fit of the gout, was to offer

Miss Eva Carthew his hand, she would drop the nephew like a hot potato, and marry him to-morrow. What do *you* say, Mrs. Colville?"

"Yes, what do *you* say?" echoed Mrs. Mellish. She had hopes in the squire's wife, a woman who never refused a soup-ticket, or a yard of flannel to one "recommended" by the rector, and appealed to her with the doubtful confidence exhibited by some heroine of melodrama when addressing "the gentler-natured" of two ruffians. "I am sure you can never be so hard on this poor girl."

Mrs. Colville drew her shawl about her, as a judge twitches his ermine before delivering judgment, and assumed a very dignified air indeed.

"My dear Mrs. Mellish, I have nothing to say against your protégée, personally; nothing whatever; she may be, as you say, the simplest of created beings. But as a woman of the world, I must say that I think a girl in her position must be very simple indeed not to understand that a bird in the hand is worth two in the bush, and to accept Lord Dirleton if he asked her. For my part, I think it is just as likely that his lordship should ask her, as that Captain Heyton will ever do so; and it is entirely on the girl's own account, and to preserve her from humiliation and disappointment, that if I were, like yourself, an intimate acquaintance of Miss Carthew's, I should think it my duty to open her eyes."

Mrs. Mellish opened her own eyes very wide indeed, dropped her little head on one side in semi-approval, and promised "to think about it;" but no further could the combined eloquence of her two visitors compel her to go.

"What do *you* think of it, my dear?" inquired she of her husband, before whom she laid the matter so soon as he came home from his parish round. He was the first rector of Dunwich that had ever worn a beard since Bishop Latimer's time, an innovation which had at first been desperately resisted. The Colvilles had called it "incongruous." Lady Wapshaw had even stigmatized it as "indecent;" but he had carried his point, and now wore moustache as well; it was literally impossible to move him from any position he took up on principle, a hair's breadth.

"What do I think of it, my dear," repeated he, stroking "the manly growth that fringed his chin," as he was wont to do when engaged in deliberation; "well, I think that Mr. Carlyle's observation with respect to the population of England being 'mostly fools,' is particularly applicable to Dunwich. Where we differ is, with respect to the public advantage likely to flow from the influence of the female aristocracy. He was really a great man—a very great man—before people of fashion began to make a fuss about him."

"My dear George, how you do fly off. I want to know what to say to Mrs. Colville and Lady Wapshaw."

"Just so, my dear; it's of them I'm thinking, for I'm quite sure it never entered into your sensible mind to speak to Eva. Of course the marriage of a girl like that with Heyton is a very serious thing. Let well alone is a very wise saying, and to bring brains into a family that have got on so uncommonly well without them for three hundred years, is without doubt a risk. But you can't tell her that without wounding her feelings on the captain's account. Besides, I do think their intelligence is growing: he is not nearly such a dunderhead as his uncle."

"But I can't tell Mrs. Colville that, George," urged Mrs. Mellish, piteously.

"Can't you? I would much sooner tell her that, than tell Eva Carthew she wasn't good enough for John Heyton. A tract on ambition, indeed! Those two women should be sent to Colney Hatch. Well, tell them that you consulted me, and that I recommended for your guidance the golden rule of life that ought to be printed in colours in every national school-room, and placed immediately beneath the ten commandments in every parish church— speaking of which reminds me that we have a vestry meeting at four, and that I must be off."

"But what *is* the golden rule?" pleaded the little woman, clinging to her husband's arm as he was about to hurry away. "I don't know what I am to tell them now."

"Now this is shocking," said the rector, kissing his wife's forehead; "this is what comes of subscribing to missionary enterprise in the Frozen Islands—yes, you did, for Lady Wapshaw showed me the half-crown in triumph; well, you may tell her from me to 'Mind Her Own Business. Colney Hatch, indeed! that woman is positively dangerous, and ought to be sent to Broadmoor."

Thus, as has been said, opinions differed in Dunwich as to the match, if match it was to be, between Miss Eva and the captain; for the little debate at the Rectory was only an example of what had taken place at twenty tea-tables every evening since the unconscious pair had been seen walking together in a certain sequestered "drive" in the park. They had met more than once, indeed, at the tables of common friends, where the captain had not failed to show a marked interest in the young lady; but that had been explained (to their own satisfaction) by the five Miss Colvilles as a momentary infatuation, and by Miss Wapshaw, even still more charitably, on the ground of the captain's delicacy of feeling. He had paid attention to her because he perceived she was of inferior social position to the other guests, just as a gentleman of fine courtesy is particular to notice his host's governess. But "those clandestine meetings in the Home Wood"—as a matter of fact the pair had met but twice, only one of which occasions had been designed—were not to be explained away. Even in a rank of society where young folks are not punctilious about the proprieties, "the young man as I walks with" is a phrase of intense significance. Imagine, therefore, the excitement that reigned in Dunwich, when it was reported that old Lord Dirleton, who rarely set foot out of his own park—and, indeed, the gout seldom permitted him to set it anywhere—had been seen to call in person at the Cedars!

CHAPTER III.

A DUEL BETWEEN PRINCIPLES.

"SHALL I go, or shall I stop?" said the doctor to Evy, as she stood with her hand upon her fluttering heart, listening for the front door to be opened to his lordship's ring. "I suppose there is no doubt what he is come about, and if you feel nervous, my dear, you shall retain your medical attendant."

It was kindly meant of the little doctor, for in his eyes Lord Dirleton was one of the greatest men upon the earth's surface. He had submitted to be sworn at by him

—to be sure the gout is an excuse for anything—on more than one occasion when he had been "called in" professionally at the hall, and had "put up with" various other indignities, as he acknowledged them to himself to be. The "nobody minds what Lord Dirleton says," which was the salve that many persons used under the like circumstances, did not prevent him from feeling galled. He felt less of a man in his lordship's company than in that of any fellow-creature, and would therefore have willingly avoided it on the present occasion. But if, as it flashed across him, Lord Dirleton was coming to speak face to face with Evy, and give her a piece of his mind, he was prepared to stand by her, at the sacrifice of never being invited to meet Sir Toby Ruffles in consultation (over his lordship's toe) again. This determination was chivalrous but unnecessary. He did the great autocrat of Dunwich wrong in supposing him capable of such an outrage. The fact was that his lordship would not have been the social tyrant he was, but for the volunteer slaves that he met with among the neighbouring population. His relation to his Dunwich neighbours had always been, thanks to themselves, that of a stick to a basket of eggs, with two exceptions; the rector was not one bit afraid of him; and in Mr. Angelo Hulet's case a cockatrice had been hatched, who ignored his authority and even his existence. If, when he had used bad words, the doctor had "stuck up to him," with "Say that again, and, damme, I'll tread on your toe"—and especially if he had carried out his threat—it would have done his lordship more good than a pint of colchicum. But such remedies lie outside the Pharmacopœia. Excellent as they are in other respects, there is no class of men so inclined to "knock under" to their social superiors as medical practitioners, which, considering that they generally catch them at a disadvantage, is inexcusable. Doctor Burne was upright enough to everybody else; but whenever he paid a professional visit—and he paid no others—to the park, he left his independence in the hall along with his umbrella.

"I am not at all afraid of Lord Dirleton," said Evy; and indeed it was not with terror of that great man that her heart went pit-a-pat. "Moreover, his visit can be scarcely intended for me."

"I don't know that," replied the doctor, suspiciously. "Hush!"

The front door bell was being "answered;" then, after a pause of a few seconds, another door below stairs was opened and closed.

"He has gone into the study to your uncle," said the doctor, taking up his hat with a sigh of relief. "God bless you, and fulfil your hope; but don't build upon it, dear Miss Evy, for I fear the old lord is not here for any good."

With a wave of his hand and a kindly smile, the doctor left the room and cautiously descended the stairs. As he passed the study, he heard voices within which seemed to him already in altercation. "By Jove!" muttered he, as he let himself out of doors, "how he'll shatter poor Hulet's nerves for him!"

Eva, alone in the drawing-room, sits huddled up in a corner of the sofa. What had her late companion meant by supposing that old Lord Dirleton had called on her account, and why should his visit bode no good to her hope? What right had the doctor to refer by implication to what she had deemed a sacred secret, but which it now seemed was one that everybody knew. Doctor Burne was correct in his surmises, no doubt, though it was so cruel of him to speak. "Dear Jack" had told her that his uncle would be sure to oppose himself to their engagement, tooth and nail, and that therefore it would be better not to disclose it, at all events at present. And now the old man had found it out. Lord Dirleton had never crossed the threshold of the Cedars before, and it could be no light thing that had brought him uninvited thither. She had seen him afar off in his family pew at church (to which her eyes had wandered in search of another object), and he had stared at her very hard, though by no means with disfavour. But he was a gentleman that looked as if he could be easily "put out," and she had Jack's word for it, that when that took place, he was "a caution." She had marked his red and swollen face, in which the blue blood of the Heytons could be so plainly discerned, and the ungloved hands that had rested on the edge of the pew, all gnarled and knotted like the trunk of a tree by his cruel malady; and she pictured him maddened and storming with the rage that she and Jack had kindled. How angry, too, would her uncle be to be informed for the first time, and by such means, of Jack's courtship! What a terrible interview must be now going on below stairs, between those men so every way antagonistic to one another, and her unfortunate self the bone of their contention, too! What a trouble she had brought upon her generous benefactor, to whom even small annoyances were wont to be a worry and a trial, beneath which his digestion easily succumbed!

Certainly Evy did not overrate the unpleasantness of that quarter of an hour which was being spent by her uncle in the study. When the doctor had left him to go upstairs, he had repaired to his medicine cupboard with the intention of recuperating himself after the fret and flutter, which the detail of his symptoms always caused him, with a dose of quinine. He had placed the bottle on the table, and had filled his glass, when there came that ring at the front door which had filled his niece with such alarm.

"Some tattling woman come to call on Evy, I suppose," was his contemptuous reflection. Whoever she was, however, his servant knew better than to admit her into his sanctum, which was tabooed to all such folk. Lady Wapshaw, indeed, armed with her subscription list for the Tonga Islanders, had on one occasion tried her right of way thither, but it was not likely she would attempt that experiment again. He had offered to give his guinea if she would subscribe a similar sum to the "Association for Compelling the Legislature to erect a Statue to Cromwell in Westminster Hall," and had favoured her with such an exposition of his political sentiments as had led her subsequently to compare him to Jack Cade. Mr. Angelo Hulet chuckled as he recalled the circumstance, and was holding the quinine up against the light, like a gourmet with a glass of yellow Chartreuse, when his door opened, and the servant announced Lord Dirleton.

The next instant, and before he could even set down his glass, this most unexpected visitor was in the room.

"*Hum. I'm not at all surprised. Drinks!*" were the first words that dropped from his lordship's lips. It was one of his peculiarities, and especially when much excited, to think aloud; his speech, however, was at no time very distinct, and this remark, though it reached the footman's ears ere he left the room, fortunately escaped those of his master. "I have called on a—um—very unpleasant business, Mr.—um."

"My name is Hulet," observed that gentleman, with dignity.

"No, no, it isn't; that wasn't the name." He drew a slip of paper, which he carried as an aid to memory, from his waistcoat pocket. "It's Carthew."

"Miss Evy Carthew is my niece," explained Mr. Hulet, frigidly.

"Just so. It's her I am come about. No, I will not take a chair."

It was plain that he would have preferred to do so, but for some social consideration, the nature of which could be guessed from his peevish and irritable tone, even if you had not caught his muttered soliloquy, "*Can't sit down with such a fellow!*"—his legs trembled under him, through weakness or passion, or perhaps from both, and he placed one gouty hand flat on the table, where it looked very like a dish of truffles, to steady himself thereby.

"Look you, sir, I have lived on good

terms with all in Dunwich for many a year, as did my fathers before me. No cause of quarrel between myself and my neighbours has ever occurred; they have kept their places, and I have kept mine. Now you are comparatively a newcomer here, and may not understand—um—ha—our respective positions."

"I understand them very well, Lord Dirleton, though the probability is we should not agree in my definition of them. A peer of the realm is, in my opinion, neither better nor worse than any other man."

"I have no wish to hear your opinions, sir," interrupted the old lord. "But if they are such as you describe them, there is all the more reason that you should listen to me. It behoves me to point out to you how absurdly impossible and absolutely out of the question it is, that anything serious can come out of this affair, upon which you are perhaps congratulating yourself. My Jack has nothing of his own to speak of, and will have nothing except what I choose to leave him. My Jack is impulsive and high-minded, it is true, but he is not a downright idiot. My Jack——"

"One moment, Lord Dirleton," interposed his companion, blandly, "I beg your pardon for interrupting you, but would you be good enough to explain yourself—to this extent at least? Who *is* 'your Jack?'"

"I—um—ha—*curse his impudence*——Sir, it is ridiculous to pretend to be ignorant of what all Dunwich has been talking about for weeks, though it came to my own ears for the first time this morning, namely, that your niece—um—*well—I suppose I must put it the other way*—that my nephew, Captain Heyton, is making love to Miss Carthew."

"Whether it seems 'ridiculous' to you

or not," replied Mr. Hulet, reddening, "or whether you choose to believe me or not, are matters quite immaterial to me, Lord Dirleton: but it is a fact that I have heard nothing whatever about this circumstance. It distresses me to hear it: excitement always makes my heart 'go'—permit me to take just half a glass of sal volatile. Well, it is but right to say that I have never heard anything to the disadvantage of 'your Jack,' as you call him; he seemed to me an inoffensive, if somewhat dull young man, with a most splendid appetite, and I have no doubt most girls would call him good looking."

"You have never looked upon him as the heir presumptive of Dunwich Park, I suppose, and heir apparent to the title, I'll wager," responded the other, sarcastically. "It is upon those grounds, however, Mr. Hulet, that I have come hither to have a few words with you. You plume yourself on being what is called 'a Radical,' I believe."

"Then you have been misinformed," was the other's curt rejoinder. "From the first moment that I began to think for myself, I have been a Republican Anabaptist."

"I did not know there was such a thing in England," observed his lordship. "I should as soon have expected to hear of an anaconda."

"There was a time, however," remarked Mr. Hulet, pointing to the picture of his ancestor above the fireplace, "when England could boast of many such; John Bradshaw, the Lord President of the Council, who condemned yonder king——"

"The devil take Bradshaw," exclaimed his lordship, irascibly—"though for that matter he must have taken him long ago—and listen to me. It may be that you are altogether out of your mind, but it also may be that you are a very cunning fellow. For argument's sake I will take you at your word, and suppose that you conceive yourself—um—*the idea of such a thing*—my equal; that birth and blood and title are all moonshine, and that a simple 'Mr.' is as good as 'my lord.'"

"If you conceive all that, you are right in every particular," rejoined the other, quietly.

"Very good. Then look you here; there can be no advantage from your point of view in your niece's marriage with my Jack; for if that happens, so sure as I stand here, nothing but my bare name shall he ever inherit from me. When I am once 'grassed in' I cannot hinder him from becoming Lord Dirleton; but not an acre of my land, not a shilling of my money, shall he ever inherit. Do I make myself intelligible?"

"You are perspicuity itself, Lord Dirleton; and if I were your family lawyer, these details of your intentions would doubtless be most interesting. I thank you for your confidence, but the disposition of your property does not concern me in any way. It seems to me a matter solely for the consideration of your Jack. My fortune is sufficient, even without the preliminary of my being 'grassed in,' to support my niece, and her husband too, in comfort; and though I make no sort of promise about the matter, if I find the young man unstained with the vices generally incidental to his position——"

Lord Dirleton's countenance was habitually purple, but it now grew black. He imagined that to be a personal reflection, which was in fact only a general censure, and the shaft went home. "Go on, sir," he gasped out; "go on."

"I say, if I find your nephew no debauchee, and that his fancy for the Turf, of which I have heard something, has not degenerated into a passion; if, in spite of his want of wits, in short, Captain Heyton turns out to be a good-hearted young fellow and a gentleman, I, for my part, as my niece's guardian and only relative, shall not oppose her choice, however much I may regret the direction it has taken."

With trembling fingers Lord Dirleton put on his hat. "I perceive I have made a mistake," said he, "in supposing you to be playing the fool, Mr. Hulet. It is impossible that any man in his senses can seriously entertain the views that you have expressed, and therefore I must believe them to have been assumed for an object. The fortune of which you have spoken is not so sufficient perhaps but that you wish to see it increased. It would have saved a great deal of time to have stated that at first, but it is a satisfaction to have reached something tangible. Jack is dear to me, I don't deny; but he has been dear to me in another sense on more than one occasion; so therefore let the ransom be reasonable. What sum will you take to withdraw Miss Carthew's pretensions to my nephew's hand?"

Mr. Hulet rose and rang the bell; the perspiration stood on his pale face, and he kept his hand pressed to his heart as though in pain.

"You shall have your answer, my lord, immediately."

It was the first time he had addressed his companion by that title throughout the interview, and the sneer with which he pronounced it was equal to a folio of contempt.

"Charles," said he, as the servant answered his summons, "show that person out of my house."

"You shall repent this, you Hulet, to

the last day of your contemptible life," gasped the old lord.

"And never let him enter it again," added Mr. Angelo Hulet ere the door closed upon his outraged visitor. "That old wretch has murdered me," groaned he as he sunk into a chair. "These palpitations will kill me outright if I don't take my prussic acid, and yet I dare not trust my hand to drop it from the bottle. As for calling Evy, the very thought of the girl brings it all back. Pit-a-pat, pit-a-pat —I'll try another glass of sal volatile. Oh, dear, oh, dear!"

CHAPTER IV.

A LOVING FAREWELL.

IT is often said that we owe a debt of gratitude to our ancestors for this and that, when it is pretty clear that they accomplished the matter in question at least as much on their own account as on ours : but there is one thing for which we have undoubtedly to thank them, as done for our especial benefit, namely, for the planting of trees of slow growth. No man, however justly proud of his constitution, can hope to get much advantage for himself out of putting acorns into the ground. All honour, then, to that early head of the house of Heyton, who caused the famous avenue in Dunwich Park—so long that the parallel lines seem almost to meet, so broad that the huge branches that fling themselves across it cannot touch by forty feet their opposite fellows—to be first " dibbled in" without hope of selfish fruition. So straight does it run, so thick are the woods on either hand of that broad green space, of which one spacious side-walk is always in grateful shadow, that you might think the avenue had been cut by skilful hands out of the solid forest, a highway to the terrestrial paradise that lies beyond it. For at the end remote from the Hall, there lay deep down in the far-stretching valley such a scene of richness and beauty as is only to be seen on English soil, with an ever-present haze in the eastern distance, which to those who had dwelt beneath it, en-hanced the glories of the rural scene ten-fold—for it marked the site of the Great City, all its roar and tumult hushed by distance. A broad grass terrace, backed by a wall of trees, extended right and left of the avenue, and commanded this fair prospect, and in the wall was many a gap, where cool green rides through ferny haunts of deer, and brakes where woodland creatures of all sorts would stand and gaze—so seldom was the Home Wood startled by bark of dog or belch of gun—crossed and re-crossed one another in no undesigned confusion, though to the casual eye without a plan.

In one of these "rides," on the afternoon of the day, the events of whose beginning we have described, a young man is pacing up and down with visible signs of impatience. He has cast his restless glance to westward, in which direction lies the village, a dozen times, and half as many has pulled out his watch, and consulted it, apparently to little purpose. It is a hunting-watch, and its gold casing has a deep dent in it, as though it had suffered from the perils of the field, otherwise there is nothing to suggest the idea of its owner being a sporting character. He is dressed in country costume, but by no means "horsily," and the only touch of foppery about him, if such it be, is the exceeding closeness with which his black hair has been cut — almost suggesting recent acquaintance with a high fever, or a gaol — and the elaborate symmetry of his small dark moustache.

A very good-looking young fellow, of three or four and twenty, as we should judge him, is our greenwood friend, though his sunburnt brow is clouded with dissatisfaction just at present, and his lips are a little compressed, as young gentlemen's who have had their own way in the world are apt to be, when their hack, or their sweetheart, are behind their time.

There is no doubt which it is on this occasion; for see, at last, from the direction of the terrace, in which he is not looking for her, trips a young girl, graceful—we will not say as a fawn, for that metaphor can scarcely have been invented by a true forester—but as a gazelle, with her large hazel eyes, soft and tender with recent sorrow, and timid with present fears.

"So, my darling, you are come at last," cries he, moving his hat at sight of her, so reverently that it seemed less in courtesy than in thankfulness to the gods that had sent him such a prize, and then moving hastily to meet her; "but you look tearful, frightened; nothing serious, I trust, has happened to detain you?"

"Nay, but there has, Jack; something very serious, and I *am* frightened, or at least I was until I met you." And then she nestled in his arms as though to be quite sure that she had found her haven.

"Which shows we ought never to be separated, my darling," observed the young man, appositely.

"And that is just what we are about to be, dear," she sobbed, "and perhaps for ever."

"My dear Evy, what is the matter? Pray, pray don't cry like that. I would rather anybody potted at me with swanshot than see your tears. You don't mean to say that your uncle has found us out, and cut up rough about it; that is impossible for anybody to do with you."

"It's impossible for *him*, Jack, that's true, for he is just the kindest soul in the world to me."

"Don't say that, Evy," pleaded the young man, tenderly; "say one of the kindest, or the other kindest."

"Of course I meant except yourself, dear; oh, pray, pray don't make fun of it all, for it's dreadful. Yes, my uncle has found us out, though that, as it happens, is nothing; but what is far worse, is that *your* uncle has found us out also."

"The devil he has!" exclaimed the captain, forgetting, in his surprise and annoyance, the tender ears of his companion; "why, how came that about? are you quite sure?"

"I am positively certain, though how it happened, or who could have told him, I have not the least idea."

"Then don't trouble yourself to look for one," observed the captain, with as much gaiety as he could assume under what was really a very serious blow to him. "It isn't like inquiring into why our marker at the butt was hit in the leg; my uncle can't find it out a second time; sooner or later he must have discovered it. Still there's no doubt it's awkward. He'll blaze up like a hill of dried heather, visible to all the country round; and it'll be hard to put him out."

"My dearest love," exclaimed Evy, sadly, "it will not only be hard, but impossible. This is the last time—I feel it—that you and I will ever meet. It is wrong of me to call you by those endearing names, to let you kiss me thus when all must be over between us. To think that yesterday we were so happy and unsuspicious, supposing that we were to meet every day alone like this, and now—ah, you will never see me more."

"And who is to prevent me, Evy?" inquired the captain, not without a flash in his dark eye that seemed to defy any one to attempt it. "If Lord Dirleton forbids us the park, the whole county doesn't belong to him, I suppose?"

"But we are going away ourselves, darling—uncle and I—at once—to-morrow, I believe."

"Going away? What, going to leave Dunwich for good?"

"Yes; at least for ever," returned Evy, dejectedly, "if that can be called for good."

"Ever is a long day," returned the young man, gravely. "Tell me all that happened, dear, from first to last, and then we will settle what is to be done. How did this sudden change in your plans first come about?"

"Well, directly after Lord Dirleton left our house——"

"Your house?" interrupted the captain, in supreme surprise. "You don't mean to tell me that he called at the Cedars?"

"Yes, indeed; he was closeted with my uncle in the study this morning for an hour or more."

"One moment, darling." A whimsical expression crossed the young man's features. "That's not the room with the family portrait in it about which Mr. Hulet talks so much, is it?"

"Yes; the one with the picture of that dreadful man with the mask and the axe; the two gentlemen seemed to have quarrelled over that even more than over poor me. So far from allowing that the Lord-President Bradshaw was a great man, as you did, and which made Uncle Angelo so pleased with you——"

"Yes; I thought he meant the man that published the Railway Guide; but no matter for that—it was a most fortunate mistake."

"Well, instead of that, I believe Lord Dirleton called him some dreadful name, and refused to listen to my uncle's political sentiments. So, beginning at that dreadful business of cutting the king's head off, things went on from bad to worse—I wish you wouldn't laugh, dear Jack, when everything is so terrible—till at last my uncle rang the bell, and told Charles to show his lordship out of doors. I saw him from the drawing-room window, and he turned back in the middle of the street, and shook his gold-headed stick at the house; his rage was something awful to witness. I believe he would have killed us all."

"Stop, stop, Evy," cried the captain, shaking with laughter, "unless you want to kill me. I would give ten pounds to have seen him, and twenty to have overheard the conversation between our respective relatives."

"Lord Dirleton called Uncle Angelo an anaconda," observed Evy, ruefully.

"A what? Oh, pray, pray don't," gasped the captain, pressing his hands to his sides. "If you only knew what my uncle's opinions were you would understand how charming all this is. He has never seen anybody worse than a Whig, and calls Lord John Russell a firebrand.

Do you think it was made quite clear to him who your uncle's great-great-grandfather really was? Oh dear, oh dear, it would have been dirt cheap at twenty pounds."

"But, Jack, don't laugh, pray don't. Indeed, this is nothing to laugh at."

"Well, well, I have done, Evy; or at least"—here was a slight relapse—"almost. There, there, I'm quite serious now. Well, after 'my noble relative,' as they say in 'the House,' left the Cedars, what happened?"

"Why, Uncle Angelo came upstairs to me; he was very shaky, poor dear, and evidently much put out, and I had to drop him some prussic acid to quiet him."

"Quiet him? Gad, I should think it did!"

"Oh, he's used to prussic acid," continued Evy, "and always takes it for his nerves. 'So, my dear Evy,' said he, when he got a little better, 'I hear you have made choice of a lover.' He didn't fly in a passion because I hadn't told him about it, but only spoke a little coldly, as though I ought to have done so, as, indeed, he well might, considering how good and kind he has always been to me. But there, you told me not to tell, you know."

"You're an angel," said Jack, admiringly, "and your uncle is a trump. Pray go on."

"Well, of course, I then told him everything; how I had often seen you, not only out at dinner in his presence, but at evening parties to which Mrs. Mellish had taken me; and how we met in the park, at first by chance, and afterwards—just once or twice—by appointment; and how good and nice you were, and how liberal you were in your opinions. I thought I would put that in, and, besides, I knew he had been pleased with you about Bradshaw.

Well, he listened very patiently, and when I had made an end of praising you (which took a long time, my darling, as you may guess), he just stooped down, and kissed my forehead."

" Like that ?" inquired the captain, with affected curiosity, and suiting the action to the word.

" No, sir, not like that ; I said 'my forehead.'"

" I beg your pardon," deprecated Jack, "like *that*, then. Well, he just stooped down and——"

"And said," continued Evy, avoiding this time this forward young gentleman's caress, "that I was a very silly girl, and did not know when I was well off. But that if I was bent upon marriage, and supposing that the object of my choice—he would keep calling you 'the object,' dear, which annoyed me very much, though I tried not to show it—supposing that you should appear to him, after due inquiry, and further personal knowledge, to be an eligible person, he would not stand in our way—with one proviso. We were not to see one another, nor even to communicate by letter, for the next six months."

"And what did you say, Evy?"

"Well, what could I say, darling? I felt that it would half kill me, but still things might have been so much worse, so after stipulating for this one interview, I promised not to meet you for six months, unless by accident. At this my uncle replied coolly that I need be under no apprehension upon that account, because we were to leave Dunwich to-morrow. Up to that time I had flattered myself that Lord Dirleton had agreed to this temporary separation between us, but my uncle then proceeded to tell me what had taken place downstairs. I will not repeat what he said of his lordship, for of course it would not be pleasant for you to hear; but he ended by protesting that he was quite certain that he should not breathe freely until at least a hundred miles were put between himself and—and—Lord Dirleton, and therefore we were to be off at once. Then my heart sank within me, darling; not because I was going away from Dunwich, nor because I feared that you would forget your Evy in six months, but on account of your uncle's anger, which my heart told me would make him bid you never see me more, and, alas, tells me still."

And once more the poor girl broke into passionate sobs, and feebly strove to prevent Jack from consoling her with his caresses.

"Things are not quite so bad as that, darling," said he, cheerfully, though, by his grave face, and the way he pulled his moustache this way and that, it was evident that he feared they would be. "And look you,

Evy," added he, solemnly, " if they come to their worst, their very worst, it would only be house and land that he could take from me, and what are they compared with you?"

"No, no," said Evy, passionately, "you must not say that. I could never be the cause of your being disinherited. It is all very well for Uncle Angelo to despise wealth and honours—and he does so quite honestly—but I know they are very dear to most men's hearts. You may think to-day that they might be well exchanged for my poor self; but you might not think so when you had lost them; and even if you did, Jack, *I* should not think so. Not a thought of this beautiful place, so full of sweet memories as it is to me (ah me, how sweet!), would come into my mind, without the bitter reflection, 'and it went from him through me.' I was wrong to come here to-day, darling. I am wrong to call you so, and yet, alas, alas, what could I do?"

It was pitiful to see her, folded in her lover's arms, but without returning his embrace, and sobbing as though her over-tried heart would break.

" Now this isn't my good, sensible Evy," reasoned the young fellow, with tender gravity, " the girl whom Doctor Burne says has more wits, and does more good with them, than all the other girls in Dunwich put together, and of whom Mrs. Mellish told me with her own lips that she wished she were a daughter of her own. I don't want to let the park slip through my fingers, you may be sure, my darling, nor the old hall, neither, for that matter. I don't pretend to any of the philosophy of your uncle, and had much rather be a great man in the sense of the vulgar herd (which is a very numerous herd indeed) than not. And on the other hand I am not going to sell my soul—*you* are my soul, you know; what ? You're not ? Then I wish you were, for then it would be something pure and good and beautiful—I am not going to sell my soul, I say, for so much gold and clay. My uncle has your taste, and likes me vastly, and I am much mistaken if he doesn't think twice before promoting my cousin Dick to the post of his heir-presumptive *vice* Jack (who married an angel). Come, look up, dear; let us 'trust in Providence,' as your uncle's friend old Cromwell used to say, 'and keep our—eyes dry.' There, I've kissed the drop away from that, and now—oh yes, I must; you can't have one dry eye and one wet one; it's contrary to nature; there, now all's right. I am dining with Lord Dirleton alone to-night—for the poor old fellow is far from well—and we shall doubtless have this out together. To-morrow morning, before you start, I will let you know what has happened. But, by-the-by, what place is it you are going to?"

"To Balcombe, I believe," sighed Evy; "a place on the south coast much recommended for the nerves."

"Balcombe, Balcombe. I have heard of that," said the captain, referring to a little volume he took from his breast pocket.

"What is that book? 'Where shall we go to this Summer,' I suppose," said Evy. "'Climate warm but bracing,' doesn't it say?"

"Not a bit of it, my dear," laughed the captain. "It is not the 'Tourist's Guide,' as you imagine. It's all about racing. Events of the year. Here it is — 'Balcombe Steeplechases, April 4th.' That's a good six months hence, and outside your uncle's limit. Well, I'll go down to Balcombe, 'by accident,' with my new Irish horse, Walltopper, and win the cup. Come, that's settled, at all events. We are just coming to the end of the Home Wood, by-the-by, dearest, and unless you prefer to wish me good-bye in public—a good-bye to last for half a year"—here followed a delicious silence, and little more was said till they parted within a few yards of the park gates, Evy a little comforted by her lover's assuring words, Jack somewhat cast down by the thought of the expected interview with his uncle, but as firm as a rock in his intention to keep his plighted word.

Mr. Angelo Hulet did the Heytons an injustice in saying that that noble race had never been famous for anything beyond descending from their ancestors; they were quite as notorious for never giving up a determination, whether for good or ill, whatever it cost them. They would as soon have thought of being persuaded out of an opinion.

CHAPTER V.

IN WHICH LORD DIRLETON OVERREACHES HIMSELF.

WHETHER the proverb, "Everybody has his good point," is one worthy of acceptance is, in our opinion, open to some doubt, since, in the case of a thoroughly offensive personage, the point in which he displays himself to less of disadvantage than others is but too often set down as a "good" one; but with respect to Lord Dirleton the saying had a a proper application enough. He was a tyrannical old Turk, highly disreputable in many ways, and venerable in none, but he was redeemed by some social virtues. He was liberal, not to say lavish, with his money; affectionate not to say amorous, in his disposition, and at least as violent in his preferences as in his dislikes. Moreover, he hated a sneak (which he shrewdly suspected his nephew Dick to be), and held a hearty plain-spoken fellow (provided that his opinions did not disagree with his own) in genuine estimation. Had it been for this reason alone, he would have liked the captain; but since the latter went also "straight as a bird" across country, was a crack shot, and his godson—the Rubric is very elastic, but never surely had it before admitted between its lines so unspiritual a sponsor as John, Lord Dirleton--"my Jack" was a prime favourite.

Moreover, some fashionable fibber had once remarked that the portrait (by young Shee) of his lordship, when a youth of eighteen, was the "image of the present

Captain Heyton," and that trifling circumstance had wonderfully assisted to increase the egotistic old fellow's affection for his eldest nephew. Jack, unlike a certain cousin of his, was not always on the look out for spoil, and never asked for his debts to be paid until the matter became pressing; didn't meddle with politics, and was not a dandy; indeed, he would have gone on active service, had not his uncle kept him at home for his own pleasure, a circumstance that gave the lad a greater claim than all else to regard himself as his heir. It would have been insufferable to most young men of any spirit to live under the same roof with Lord Dirleton in a position of dependence upon him; but it was not so with Jack, who really liked his uncle, and would as soon have thought of playing the sycophant as the piano. Bashaw as he was to most folks, Lord Dirleton thoroughly understood that Jack's own liberties were never to be encroached upon, nor Jack himself dictated to *de haut en bas ;* and that, sooner than submit to the least insult, the young fellow would have packed up his half-dozen portmanteaus of fashionable garments, and left the hall at once, to face the world on his own trumpery five hundred a year. And what would his lordship have done then? Who would have understood his humours, and attended to his wants as Jack had done? Who would have " managed " him when he had the gout, so as to keep his temper within reasonable bounds, and prevent the servants from leaving the house *en masse ?* Who would haves uperintended his stud, and had the pedigree of every horse at his finger-ends, as well as the names of the winners of all the Derbys, which formed the calendar of his own past? " Let me see, when was it I first sat for Loamshire, Jack?" or " Ran away with that Italian woman?" or " Went out with Sir Harcourt Leslie?" To each of which queries Jack would answer without error, as he quietly cracked his walnuts, "Blisbury's year," or "Archimedes' year," or "The Dead Heat year, between Antimony and Perspiration," just as it happened. Who but Jack would have left the billiard-room that winter's night, in his pumps and silk stockings, and gone into the Home Wood after those infernal poachers, and netted the whole lot of them? Well, certainly not Dick, who, what with his lisp, and his flute, and his French phrases, might as well have been his niece as his nephew.

And if Jack was not without a sense of the "necessity" that he had made himself —not with calculating design, however— to the old man, he also acknowledged in his uncle, not, indeed, a patron, but a most generous and kindly benefactor. He was not afraid of Lord Dirleton—he was afraid of no man—but he had carefully avoided all occasions of quarrel with him, and now that a disagreement was impending between them—and one likely to be most serious and lasting—his pity for himself was not unmingled with pity for his antagonist. "The old fellow has always behaved to me like a trump," was his present reflection, as he took his way slowly towards the hall, after his parting with Evy, "and whatever he says, I will try to keep my temper, and look at the matter from his own point of view." He meant, of course, short of yielding the main point, of which, as we have said, he was, by birth, incapable. Even his cousin Dick, by comparison a most prudent and calculating character, never gave up a fancy, no matter what the pecuniary advantage of so doing.

Unfortunately Lord Dirleton himself was a Heyton also.

Never had the park, with its herds and

flocks, seemed so well worth possessing as now, when the captain trod it, as its heir presumptive, perhaps for the last time; never had the grand old hall seemed an inheritance so fair as now, when he was approaching it as its future master, perhaps for the last time. To ordinary visitors on foot, the porter, a solemn being, resplendent in scarlet and gold, opened the postern door let in to one side of the huge gateway; to persons of higher quality, and to junior members of the house of Heyton, one wing of the gate was thrown back at their approach; for his lordship and the captain alone was reserved the honour of having the great gate thrown open.

In the first case the resplendent creature, wrapt in contemplative calm, took no notice of the incomer, whom he ushered into the courtyard, there to be received by an inferior member of the household; in the second he stood bolt upright, like a soldier at "attention;" in the third case he removed his gold-bound and cockaded hat, and bowed to the extreme limit that obesity permitted. "Will old Benson ever bow like that again to me?" thought Jack, grimly, as he acknowledged this retainer's profound salutation. For the entail stopped with the present lord, who had, as has been said, the power of leaving house, and land, and gold, everything, in fact, but his bare title, to whomsoever he pleased. Jack's mind pursued the same thread of thought —not a very high one, perhaps, but a natural one enough under the circumstances —as he mounted the great stairs, up which he had so often assisted his uncle's crippled feet, and passed along the gallery from whose walls his ancestors seemed to regard him with doubtful looks. "This is not the young man that is to succeed us, then, after all," whispered they to one another.

In his own apartments, where he proceeded to dress himself for dinner, there were many things to suggest a continuance of the same theme. The sitting-room had been fitted up by his uncle, as a "surprise" to him, on some occasions of his own absence, in the manner that had been judged suitable to the young man's taste; the furniture was of oak, carved in imitation of various incidents of the chase, and on the walls, in frames similarly carved, were engravings of the most famous pictures in connection with that subject. His dressing-table, again, was weighted with the most splendid articles of the toilet in gold or silver, all gifts from that loving kinsman, whose affection he was now about to try to the uttermost, and, in all probability, beyond what it could bear. But though a sigh would now and then escape Jack on his own account, his chief regret was still, as before, for him who had loaded him with so many tokens of his love, and in whose eyes the return he was about to make for them must needs seem heartless and ungrateful.

"If I am kicked out of this," mused the captain, not in self-conceit, but with the air of one who states a fact to be regretted, "the poor old fellow will find himself very lonely, I am afraid." And then the gong sounded for dinner.

His unwonted pedestrian expedition to the village, and the excitement of his interview with Mr. Hulet, had already brought his lordship's leg to the foot rest, which Jack did not fail to remark upon with becoming solicitude, and not only on his relative's account, but on his own, for he well knew that the circumstance would not be in his favour in the coming struggle.

"Yes," replied his uncle, peevishly, "I've been most infernally worried to-day, and worry always flies to my toe."

This was the fact, and his lordship was

apt to insist upon it, as a reason why he should never be thwarted, just as Mr. Hulet, equally autocratic, though on a smaller scale, objected to contradiction on the ground that "it made his heart go." Jack dared not ask what had worried his noble relative, lest he should blurt out something before the servants, but merely expressed his regret; and the dinner proceeded in total silence, except that his lordship "broke out" occasionally (wholly without occasion) at the cook; and that also was a bad sign.

No sooner were they left alone together, however—the claret with Jack, and the whisky, medicinally prescribed, beside his uncle—than the latter drew a letter from his waistcoat pocket, and tossed it over to his companion, with a "Read that, sir."

Jack obeyed him, and then, with a quiet face, returned it.

"Well, what have you to say to it, sir?"

"Nothing more, uncle, than what is usually said of anonymous communications. It is a very blackguard trick, if such a phrase can be used in the case of a female, for I am afraid the handwriting reveals the sex."

"Yes, it's a woman of course," answered his lordship. "'A true friend to the social proprieties ventures to ask Lord Dirleton whether he is aware that his nephew, Captain Heyton, is on the verge of being entangled into a matrimonial engagement by the niece of Mr. Angelo Hulet, a Miss Carthew?' No man could have written like that. But that is not the point, sir. What I wish to inquire is, is it true?"

"So far as the being 'entangled in a matrimonial engagement,' is concerned, uncle," replied the young man, slowly, "it is a lie. Otherwise the statement is correct enough."

"I don't quite understand you, Jack," answered his lordship, brightening up. "I am not very straightlaced, as you know; but I do hope that you have not been so imprudent—in the village here, close under my very nose—to form any connection that——"

"My lord, I must beg you not to finish that sentence," interrupted Jack, with a sudden flush on his face. "Miss Carthew is a lady born and bred, in all respects my equal—in most my superior. My denial referred only to the word 'entangled;' she is utterly incapable of such conduct as that infamous letter would attribute to her."

"Very likely; but you don't mean to tell me that you have engaged yourself to this girl?"

"Well, if you ask me, uncle, I must needs reply, yes."

"You must, must you?" roared the old man, making, as though he would strike the table with his fist, and remembering his gout only just in time to avert the most frightful consequences, "then, by the Lord Harry, you need not trouble to call me 'uncle' any more."

"Very good, my lord."

Here the young man concluded his task of peeling some half-dozen walnuts, and placed them on his companion's plate, as he had been wont to do at dessert-time, in the walnut season, for many a year. In the spring he peeled oranges for him in the form of an hour-glass.

"I don't want your walnuts," said his lordship, peevishly, yet evidently touched by the accustomed action nevertheless. "I want you to show a little common sense, and to remember your position."

"I do not forget it, my lord," returned Jack, modestly. "It has been a very comfortable one, thanks to you, for many years."

"Well, then, why not keep it, sir? Why quarrel with your bread and butter—nay, your bread, for you have almost nothing of your own—for the sake of a pretty face. You are aware I can leave my money just as I please. I've got neither wife nor children"—perhaps the ghost of a smile flickered on his nephew's lip, or perhaps the old lord only imagined it—but he added, hastily, "that is to speak of. All that you inherit, independent of my favour, is a barren title; and can there be anything more wretched than the position of a pauper peer? You will, of course, have a lot of brats, and be unable to maintain them; for what government will give its loaves and fishes in return for a mere vote without influence. But there, I am talking to one who doubtless never troubles himself to look so far ahead. Let me speak, then, of the present. Would you like to be dependent on the bounty of such a father-in-law as Mr. Angelo Hulet; for that, as he informed me with his own lips, is the fate that is in store for you. Have you ever seen that man, sir? heard him talk?"

"I have met him on one or two occasions," replied Jack; "he is not a man to my taste, of course, but he is a gentleman; and——"

"A gentleman, begad!" broke in the old lord; "the devil he is! Then I don't know what a gentleman means. Are you aware, to begin with, that he is descended —and boasts of it, sir, boasts of it—from that cut-throat villain, Hulet, who beheaded Charles the First? He's got a picture of him in his parlour, to which he pays as much adoration as any Papist to an altar-piece. Do you suppose I would ever give my permission to cross the Heyton stock with that of a regicide? No, sir, upon my honour I never will; so there.

And I tell you what. You shan't have the title neither; and I'll let the girl know this, since that's what she's after, I suspect; for if you marry her, I'll marry too, begad I will, and beget heirs, like my fathers before me; so there."

In spite of the evil turn affairs were taking, Jack could not repress a smile at this characteristic menace.

"Of course, my lord," replied he, quietly, "you will act as you think proper. The young lady in question is not, however, let me remind you, a Hulet; but the daughter of an officer of distinguished merit."

"Um! ha! they're always that," soliloquized Lord Dirleton; "the only child of a hard-working clergyman, who succumbed beneath his own parochial labours, or else of an officer of high rank, who perished upon the blood-stained field. Who ever knew a mésalliance without them. However," added he, "she comes of the Hulet blood on one side; and that is quite enough for me. These are revolutionary times, sir; I should not be surprised—what's bred in the bone, you know, is sure to come out in the flesh—if some offspring of this projected union should become headsman to the future Cromwell. Oh, Jack, Jack!" exclaimed the old lord, with a sudden descent from historical prediction to the lowly level of natural affection, "why should you be such a damned fool? My word is passed, you know, upon this subject, and I can't draw back, even if I would——"

"And *my* word, my lord, is also given," interposed Jack, with dignity; "so with your leave we will let the matter drop. It is from no want of dutifulness, nor of gratitude, believe me, that I am compelled to take a course which I feel must dissever my future from yours. You have been a father to me ever since I lost my own—more indulgent than most fathers, and as kind——"

"And as loving," put in the old lord, in trembling tones—"as loving as any father, you ungrateful dog."

"Indeed I do believe it, sir," confessed Jack, playing nervously with his claret glass, "and I am not ungrateful. What I would persuade you, if I could, is, that in giving up all you have to give me, I shall feel the loss of your love the most of all."

"Then why give it up, Jack?" pleaded the other; "or if you will be so infernally obstinate, at least, there need be no hurry about giving it up. You are not going to marry this girl to-morrow, I suppose, nor yet the next day?"

Jack, with a certain comical air of chagrin, admtted that such was the fact.

"Very well, then," continued the old lord, "don't let us say another word about it at present; that is, after I have asked one favour of you, and you have granted it."

It touched Jack much to hear his uncle, who had been so long accustomed to lay down the law to everybody, thus appealing almost as a suppliant, and to him.

"Indeed," said he, "there is nothing, my lord, in which I will not oblige you, short of giving up what has become the dearest object of my life."

"Then promise me not to see this young lady for the next twelve months," said Lord Dirleton, grimly.

Jack had stepped into the pitfall. It was an ungenerous advantage for his uncle to have taken, and that the old man felt it to be so was evident from the apologetic tone in which he went on to speak.

"This will be a good touchstone of the sincerity of your affections, you see, Jack; if you are really so bewitched as to be past cure, absence will only make you the more foolish—I mean, more fond; whereas, if your attachment is but a passing fancy, as I most sincerely trust it may prove to be, you will forget all about the girl during the interval. Come, you can't be worse for waiting—though h'm—ha—he shall be no better; for I'm fixed as the poles about the main point—and you did say you would accede to my request."

"Nay, my lord," said Jack, who felt much aggrieved by this sharp practice, "I spoke with the tacit understanding that you would ask something in reason. Now, if you made it six months——"

"Pooh, pooh. Six months is nothing; I've loved a girl myself for as long as that. Let us say nine. In a subject of this delicate nature there's an appropriateness in nine. H'm—ha—begad, if it ain't like a Dutch auction. Come, say nine."

"It must be six months, my lord," said

Jack, speaking with great gravity, yet scarcely able to repress a smile, not at his lordship's "aside," but at the reflection that he was hoisting his adversary with his own petard; for was he not already banished from the beloved object for the time in question?

"Well, well, let us say six, Jack; h'm— in six months this young fool will have come to his senses; only mind this, the separation between you must be complete. You must not even write to one another; I'll have no sending kisses in sealing-wax."

"That is a very hard stipulation," pleaded Jack. He was by nature the reverse of hypocritical; and if his uncle had not laid that trap for him, he would have at once confessed that Mr. Hulet had already made this very proviso: but now he had no scruples.

"Come, come; no meetings and no correspondence for six months, sir," insisted his lordship, impatiently. "Promise me that!"

"Very good, my lord," said Jack, submissively. "I will send but one note to Miss Carthew this morning to tell her how the matter stands, and then I will neither see nor write to her again for the next half year."

"Good lad, good lad," answered the old man, approvingly; "and look here, Jack, you need not trouble yourself during that interval to call me 'my lord' any more. And—um—he—this folly of his will never last so long; three months was the extreme limit with me, though I did tell him six. Yes, and now I'll eat your walnuts."

CHAPTER VI.

BALCOMBE.

THERE is no country in the world, prone as our fellow-countrymen are to travel abroad in pretended search of the picturesque, of such various beauty as old England. Almost every one of its inland counties has its characteristic charm; while its sea-coast is absolutely inexhaustible for variety of form and colour.

As to Dunwich, I positively assert that there is nothing to compare with it for rich repose and home-like splendour in the four quarters of the globe, and yet Dunwich is not (I am glad to say) "a show place" by any means. "I trust we have within this realm" fifty such tranquil paradises, on which no sooner do our eyes rest than we exclaim, "Here should I like to dwell."

Now Balcombe *is* a show place. All who can read the announcements of the railway companies upon the walls, with respect to family excursion tickets, have read of it, and everybody who is anybody (that is, about one thousandth part of our total population) has visited it. Especially everybody with nerves. Balcombe is situated on a beautiful bay on the south coast, where the trees start from the very edge of the shore, on quite an Alpine expedition. They climb seven hills, among which, in dells, and clefts, or on commanding "spurs," the town is set, and from this circumstance it is sometimes called the British Babylon. It has no other affinity, however, with the Scarlet Woman, who, indeed, is held in general abomination at Balcombe, the migratory population of which—and that is the only population worth talking about—are, as in most seaside places of fashionable resort in England, eminently evangelical. There is something in the ocean air, I fancy, that is inimical to Popery, or perhaps it is the iodine in the seaweed, or the smell of the shrimps. Nor is the morality of Balcombe, as a rule, inferior to its orthodoxy, though this may be in some measure accounted for by physical causes. Five-sixths of its visitors are confirmed invalids, and persons who go about with respirators in bath-chairs, seldom indulge in loud language, and almost never frequent music halls or casinos. If a "Hall by the Sea," such as there is at Ramsgate, and other places, patronized by the hale and vulgar, was to be set up at Balcombe, it would fail most miserably, though it would doubtless have its effects; the very idea of it, the issuing of its prospectus, would be fatal to many; the mere laying its lance in rest would probably empty half the bath-chairs. A shock of that kind would be too much for the poor folks with nerves. I have heard many persons thus afflicted positively find fault with the beauty of Balcombe, because of its attracting "mobs of people" during the summer months, and when an excursion train is announced they all withdraw into their villas like rabbits in a warren, and keep themselves *to* themselves, till the invaders have worked their wicked wills and departed. Thus it was not for its beauty of situation, nor for its fashionable society, nor even for the far-famed table d'hôte to be found at its principal boarding-house, Lucullus Mansion, that Mr. Angelo Hulet visited Balcombe, but for its climate and "aspects," which last—to judge by its guide-book, edited by "a distinguished physician"—were (one or other of them) beneficial to every description of human malady.

On Number One hill you found a more certain cure for dyspepsia than even the Revalenta Arabica; on Number Two the coats of the stomach were renovated as quickly as any old "swallow-tail" subjected to the tailor's iron; on Number Three you took your stand—or were enabled to take it after a day or two—and defied gout; on Number Four, though you might have arrived there speechless from bronchitis, in a few weeks you could communicate verbally with your friends on the pier below without the aid of a speaking-trumpet; and so on. But all the seven hills and all their "aspects" were equally good for the nerves. To a hale and hearty stranger, indeed, arriving in this recuperating spot for the first time, the idea was apt to occur to him that it was raining. Between myself and the reader, I may remark

that it does rain at Balcombe six days out
of every seven, and is very near doing it on
the seventh ; but this the inhabitants deny.
All the people with nerves, and all the
people with gout, and all the people with
indifferent coats to their stomachs—everybody, in fact, except the consumptive pa-
tients—come out in the rain without um-
brellas, and protest that there is " nothing
falling," not even the barometer. It is
a very warm and gentle rain, no doubt,
but it wets you very thoroughly unless you
have a waterproof, and my suspicion is
that these boastful cripples, like the gentleman who didn't mind fighting duels because he had a shirt made of chain armour,
wear waterproofs under their clothes. And
yet they are no perjurers, for just as an
Irishman (when he is well away from it)
paints his own country in all honesty as an
agreeable dwelling-place, so they believe
what they say. There is an esprit de corps

among the Balcombe invalids, which compels them to swear through thick and thin by their adopted home, and to take the guide-book by the "distinguished physician" (a most dexterous manipulator of the statistics of rain-fall) as gospel. Nay, the local enthusiasm seizes even upon their new recruits, and no sooner did Mr. Angelo Hulet find himself located at Lucullus Mansion, than he pronounced himself "quite another man." He had evidently, however, no intention of dispensing with his former infallible remedies in the way of drugs and potions, for he had already set them out in his own apartment, in admirable disorder, and taken a good pull at a tonic made of dandelions, and much recommended after travel. Thus refreshed, he sat down at the open window, and looked out on sky, and sea, and shore with a sentimental air; it was enjoined by the label on the dandelion bottle to keep himself quiet after taking that subtle essence, but it was not on that account that he sat so still and thoughtful.

Mr. Angelo Hulet had visited Balcombe —not for its "aspects," nor its climate— nearly forty years ago, when he was young and vigorous, and never needed so much as a glass of sherry and bitters to give him "a tone;" when his head was covered with curling locks, that required no careful arrangement of the comb to hide his baldness; when his hand was steady with his gun among the stubble, and only trembled at the touch of beauty; when—

> "——Ah, doleful When
> That marked the change 'twixt now and then !"

How aptly could he have gone on to quote:

> "This breathing house not built with hands,
> This body that does me grievous wrong,
> O'er airy cliffs and glittering sands,
> How lightly Then it flashed along !
> Nought cared this body for wind nor weather,
> When Youth and I lived in't together !"

Mr. Angelo Hulet had never been given to poetry even in his youth, but something like the foregoing was in his mind as he regarded the unchanging sea by which he had wandered nearly half a century before, not without a meet companion. The thoughts of forty years ago, indeed, are enough to make a poet of an attorney.

In the next room to his own sat Evy, looking on the same fair sights, but with far other thoughts. Her hand clasped Jack's last letter, the one in which he had bidden farewell to her for six months, but in hopeful words. The old lord had refused his consent indeed, but on the whole had received the news of his engagement with more patience than he had anticipated. Time might do much for them; and meanwhile, though forbidden to speak or write, his dream by night, his thought by day, would be of his darling Evy. She tried to believe this, or at all events to believe that he would not forget her, or be false to her, but it was hard to do so, for she was a very sensible young woman. She well knew that, even among men, not three in a thousand were like her uncle, uninfluenced by the attractions of social position, and that among women the proportion was even less; that every young lady in Dunwich was setting her cap—or her chignon—at the captain; and that wherever he went the heir-presumptive of Lord Dirleton would be the object of matrimonial ambition. True, she had won his heart—a feat that in her modesty she thought astonishing; but was it not likely that some other, fairer, nobler, better than she, would win it from her? Her uncle evidently thought so; deemed that this young man's love was but a passing fancy, or he would not have imposed this ordeal of separation; and Jack's uncle thought the same. She should always love him, of course; she would carry that little locket with his hair in it, that she was now covering with kisses, to the grave; but was it to be expected that he would be equally faithful? Kind-hearted Mrs. Mellish had hinted to her by delicate indirect allusion to the necessity of finding happiness in one's own home, that it was not to be expected' and Doctor Burne had told her so more plainly. The rector only had given her comfort.

For in their "good-byes" they had all spoken of the matter without reserve. "Jack has a sound heart, my dear," Mr. Mellish had whispered in her ear, "and will never prove a snob." A snob, indeed! No, that was impossible; but without showing himself in that light it was very possible that he might repent of his hasty engagement, or be persuaded by his uncle to have a due regard to his own interests, which indeed she had herself besought him not to sacrifice on her account. She was not sorry to come away from Dunwich — a place she had once wished to live and die in, and which to her mind had still no equal. Its own surpassing beauty seemed indeed now doubled, tinged as it was with the hues of first love.

> "From end to end
> Of all the landscape underneath,
> There was no place that did not breathe
> Some gracious memory"—

of him. But it would have been terrible to remain there with him so near, and yet forbidden to see him. She did not expect to find pleasure in Balcombe, but at all events it would be without the pain of fond regret. And how very, very beautiful it looked in that autumn evening! Lucullus Mansion was an edifice of considerable pretension, standing in its own grounds, with a stone terrace round three sides of it, and a lawn called "the garden," and which would really have been a garden, but that it was so steep that the flower beds, that ran down to the sea, from which it was separated only by a low wall, could not stick on to it, but were washed away by the unceasing drizzle. To the eastward lay the open ocean dotted with a large white sail or two, and with a whole fleet of little red ones, which were the fishing boats bound for home. On the south was the harbour, a scene of lively movement and harmonious sound.

Evy's glance wandered listlessly from one fair object to another for some minutes, then she sighed and took out a little book on which her eyes rivetted themselves with a very different expression. It was not a poem on which they were fixed, though they grew soft and tender; it was not a prayer, though there was something of devotion in them; it was a mere date and a few words extracted from a racing calendar :

"April 4th, Balcombe steeplechases."

She was still gazing on this memorandum when there came a knock at the door, and a female voice was heard asking in persuasive accents, permission to enter: "My dear young lady," it said, "may I— I'm Mrs. Hodlin Barmby — come in?" But though Evy answered "Yes," Mrs. Hodlin Barmby is much too important a personage to be introduced at the end of a chapter.

CHAPTER VII.

A NEW PROFESSION.

READER, have you ever lived in lodgings? If so, you cannot fail to have observed that your landlady is in the enjoyment of all those "Woman's Rights" for which so many of her sisterhood are so vainly clamorous; that her domestic sway is supreme, and that her husband is very literally "nowhere." If you see him at all (which is unusual), it is always in a subordinate capacity; if you hear him address his wife—"answer" her in the sense that that "hussey," the servant girl understands the phrase, he never does—it is in meek and deferential accents. Under the course of treatment to which he is subjected, he not seldom succumbs altogether, which is why so many landladies are widows; but if he lives, he plays second fiddle in the matrimonial duet. If, being yourself a lady, and interested in the triumphs of your sex, you inquire of his wife how this most desirable state of things has been brought about, she will plump down, uninvited, on the nearest chair, begin to rock herself to and fro, and presently burst into tears. "He'd need do all he could, ma'am," she explains, "and never cross me in anything while the breath is in him, for when I married him, I was well-to-do in the world, and he has brought ruin upon me."

It may have been drink, or it may have been a passion for bagatelle, or even skittles (for some men are very low in their tastes); but he has spent her money, and surely the least he can do in reparation is to constitute himself her slave. In China the villain would probably have lost himself, after all else was gone, to some antagonist at cards or dice; but that being impossible in a civilized country, his services are his ruined wife's—" and very little use, heaven knows, he is to me."

Now Lucullus Mansion was a glorified lodging-house, the very pink and perfection of one, but still a lodging-house—and what holds good of the least holds good of the lordliest, in such cases; its mistress, Mrs. Hodlin Barmby, had been ruined by the husband over whom she now reigned. This mischance had not been owing to bagatelle, nor yet to skittles. Mr. Hodlin Barmby was a gentleman by birth and taste, and had lost his wife's money where he had lost his own, years before, in a gentlemanly way, on Epsom Downs. He was the younger son of a baronet, and had had but four thousand pounds to lose, but such was his impulsive nature and so broad his views, that he would have got rid with equal facility of forty thousand. The loss of his own patrimony affected him very little, but that of his wife's went to his heart. "My dear," said he, on the evening of that fatal Derby, "I have been a selfish scoundrel. You have only to endorse that statement, and I'll blow out my——"

"Stop, Charles!" cried his wife imperatively (up to that hour she had been the mildest of women, and permitted him to have his own way in everything). "You have shown that there is nothing of that description to blow out; there is no use in crying over spilt milk, but henceforth, permit me to manage matters. Will you do as I tell you, and let me hold our purse-strings in case there may be one day anything in it?"

"My dear," said he, with all the solemnity of which he was master, "with all my worldly goods—if I ever have any—I thee endow. It is true I said that once before; but the obligations of the marriage service have a certain legal compulsion about them, like a tradesman's bill, which is offensive to a man of honour; this time you have my word as a gentleman. Henceforth I am entirely in your hands."

"Very good, Charles," rejoined his wife, who never gave him one word of reproach for having ruined her, except what was implied in that form of address; up to that time she had always called him "Charley," but henceforth that playful diminutive was denied to him; the position she designed for him did not permit of it. "Very good, Charles; I feel confident you will never repent it. You are doubtless surprised at my receiving your bad news so coolly, but the fact is, the catastrophe is only what I expected would happen sooner or later, even at the moment when I accepted you."

"The deuce you did!" exclaimed her husband.

"Yes, Charles," she went on, "a woman is always a fool when she is in love; but she is not always unconscious of the fact. However, as I say, I knew you would come to grief, as you had done before, and I laid my plans for this emergency long ago. I don't say, mind, that they will recover the twenty thousand you dropped on Epsom Downs to-day—but if they succeed as I expect they will do, they will enable us to live in comfort."

"That would be more than I deserve," said Mr. Hodlin Barmby, meekly.

"Listen, Charles. You are not a clever man, but you are very nice. Everybody likes you, and would do anything for you, if they could, short of dipping their hands into their pockets——"

"I shouldn't like them to do that," put in Mr. Barmby, reddening.

"You have nothing to do with it, sir," replied the lady, firmly. "Please to remember that it is I who am manager now. As it happens, however, we are agreed upon this point—I do not intend to be under obligations to anybody. Let us add up our assets. You have, on your side, social popularity and some judgment in wines and horses. I, on my part, understand how to keep house, to give really good dinners, and to set people at ease with one another. Now you, and many persons who have money to spare, have often told me that at the very best hotels—as they are at present managed—you get nothing fit to eat and are half poisoned by the wines. The master and mistress, being themselves only fourth-rate people, cannot of course be expected to know what persons of position are accustomed to in their own houses, and are only bent on getting so much a head out of every meal."

"Good gracious!" ejaculated her husband, arranging his shirt-collar, "we are going to keep an inn. I see the sign before my eyes. The Pig and Periwinkle. Hodlin Barmby; licensed retailer of spirits."

"No, Charles, we are not. If you were a wiser man, we might, indeed, take the Star and Garter at Richmond, and make our fortune; but I anticipated your conventional objections to such a scheme. We must content ourselves with a fashionable boarding-house. You will superintend the wine department, look after the men-servants, and preside at the table d'hôte. As the son of a baronet—to which circumstance you must make constant allusion—you will attract the small deer in crowds; while our own friends will rally round us, at first for our own sake, and afterwards because they will find themselves ten times more comfortable at Lucullus Mansion than elsewhere. I fixed on the name six months ago, ever since you told me you had put the 'pot' on Lucullus, who, Lord George informed me, was named after a Roman gourmand. The house is that large hotel that we stayed at during our honeymoon at Balcombe, and which has been advertised for sale these three weeks. Of course, we can't buy it, but I have no doubt I can make some arrangement for carrying it on for the next year or so."

"But where is the money to come from, my good woman?"

"The money, sir? Do you know how Rothschild made his money? Entirely by confining himself to his own affairs. Pray don't let me have to remind you for the third time of the change in our positions."

And thus it was that Mrs. Hodlin Barmby became the tenant of Lucullus Mansion. Some say an uncle of hers who had made his fortune in trade, and had looked very coldly on her in her days of prosperous dissipation, lent her the money for this useful purpose; others assert that she had always kept a few hundred pounds of her own against that "rainy day" which she had foreseen only too clearly; and one or two scandalous persons will have it that it came from Lord George. To these last I give the lie direct. Mrs. Hodlin Barmby was as honest as she was pretty, and Lord George Despard was as poor as he was unprincipled—a comparison which to those who know him implies that he had not a single penny. His "countenance," however, was invaluable to the new speculation, of which he good-naturedly appointed himself tout in ordinary; and he even brought Lady George herself—with whom he was not accustomed to travel—to shed a social lustre on the establishment in its first season. By this time, thanks to the tactics of its female manager, it was a very thriving concern, and most deservedly so. Living, indeed, was far from cheap at Lucullus Mansion, but on the other hand it was not only good, but excellent. The gravy soups did not remind you of beef-tea. The entrées were to be eaten, not passed untasted; the wines (even the port) were to be drunk, and nothing was to be avoided save the taking too much of them. The house was always full during the two seasons of which Balcombe boasted, and which extended respectively from the beginning of November to the end of April, and from the beginning of May to the end of October, and Mr. Hodlin Barmby was never without a ten-pound note in his pocket to spend as he pleased. He kept his word to his wife; never disobeyed her; never interfered with her arrangements; and always "knew his place," which, when not at the head of his table d'hôte, was a very subordinate one. At the same time he was not without his uses. Disagreeable things will happen even in the best regulated households; gentlemen sometimes came to the mansion who fancied that their length of purse permitted them to find fault without occasion, and to take other unaccountable liberties. To these Mr. Barmby presented in person a printed card with the following inscription: "H. B., presents his compliments to ——, and while thanking him for his past patronage begs respectfully to decline a continuance of it after to-morrow at noon, at which hour Number — (the apartment of the offender) has been bespoken by a *gentleman*."

Mr. Hodlin Barmby was six feet two in his stockings, besides being, as we have already hinted, the son of a baronet, and this combination of physical and moral force never failed in its desired effect. If any lady misconducted herself, or (as happened once or twice) arrived as a privateer under the false colours of respectability, Mrs. Hodlin Barmby needed no assistance to settle that little matter; she was five feet ten in her—well in her evening shoes, and the co-heiress of a most respectable county clergyman, who had made forty thousand pounds in mines; and if one of these two female antagonists happened to be taken with hysterics, it was never Mrs. H. B., let me assure you, but the other.

And yet upon ordinary occasions nothing could be more agreeable and even winning than the excellent hostess of Lucullus Mansion. When she entered our heroine's apartment now, in answer to the latter's courteous "Pray come in," Evy thought she had never beheld a handsomer or more kindly-looking woman.

"Pardon this intrusion, Miss Carthew," said she, "but it is my duty, as your landlady, to ask whether you have all you want—you are dressed, I see. Else if I could have helped you, I should have been very glad. One never gets proper attention from one's own maid on the first day of one's arrival anywhere—or at least that used to be my experience, when I kept a maid."

Evy's own personal attendant had in fact been so occupied in getting her tea, and making her acquaintances below stairs, that she had neglected to visit her young mistress until she was far advanced with her toilet, and occupied as Evy was with her own tender thoughts, she had declined her services and dismissed her.

"I have got on very well Mrs. Barmby, thank you," said Evy; "and find everything very nice, quite as nice as in one's own home, just as your old friend Mrs. Mellish told me I should do. By-the-by, I have a note for you from her, which in the hurry of our arrival I forgot to give you downstairs."

While Mrs. Barmby read it, Evy took stock of her, as women are wont to do of one another. How tastefully, yet quietly, she was dressed; and what a perfect lady she looked in that gray silk trimmed with black lace, an attire rather too matronly perhaps for so young a woman—she was not more than thirty-two at worst—but still that was a fault on the right side. She would grow too stout in time, doubtless, but at present, her figure was splendid, and if all that beautiful hair was her own —and it really looked as if it was—she had more than Evy herself had, though being of a lighter brown, it made less show. What long lashes her eyes had, and—but, surely they were wet with tears!

Evy was not mistaken, there was something in that little note which had set stout Mrs. Barmby crying.

"It must seem very foolish, dear Miss Carthew," explained she, "for a person in my position to give way to sentiment, but I have not seen Mary Mellish—she was Mary Newcombe then—for these fifteen years. We were great allies at school, and it was not likely that I should forget her, of course; but I didn't expect her to remember *me*, or at all events to write so very kindly. Such things don't happen to me every day, I assure you. 'You must make a friend of her—that's of you, Miss Carthew,' Mary says, 'for my sake!' May I?"

"I am sure, Mrs. Barmby, I hope you will," said Evy, earnestly.

"Did Mrs. Mellish tell you about me—I mean about my little antecedents—my dear?"

"Yes," said Evy, blushing.

"Come, that's a comfort," exclaimed the other, simply. "I know it's very weak and foolish in me, but I do like ladies who come here to know something about who I was. Not that I was anything to boast of, but only that they shouldn't ask me, so very sharply at the outset, whether the beds are aired, and if there isn't some reduction in our charges in case they have their luncheons out. Of course *you* wouldn't have done it; my instinct told me that you were just what Mary describes you to be, and seeing you so young and winsome—just such a one, I thought, as the only child we ever had might have grown up to be by this time, had she lived—I made bold to come and see you in your room, my dear."

"That was very kind of you," said Evy, "and, to tell the truth, I was rather alarmed at the prospect of going down to the table d'hôte, without knowing anybody there."

"You shall sit next to me, my dear, and

your uncle shall be on the other side of you, if you please," said Mrs. Barmby, assuringly, "though I did intend it to be the other way, in which case you would have had Mr. de Coucy for your neighbour, a most charming old gentleman. He will probably propose to you in a day or two, but you must not mind that."

"But I think I shall mind it very much!" ejaculated Evy, with unfeigned alarm.

"Oh, no, you won't, when you have seen a little of him. It's only a way he has with all young ladies; and when you have refused him—as of course you will do—it will not make a bit of difference in his pleasant talk (for he is a most agreeable man), and it will only amuse you the more to see him laying siege to somebody else. He is a thorough gentleman at heart, besides being very well connected; he's first cousin to Lord Dirleton, who lives in your neighbourhood, by-the-by, and whom you doubtless know."

"I have seen him," said Evy, conscious that she was growing very red; "but I cannot say I know him.—Will there be many people at the table d'hôte to-day?"

"Well, my dear, about fifty." Mrs. Barmby took out a slip of paper, with a list of names very neatly written out, and referred to it. "Yes; there are fifty-three, which, unless somebody omits to come at the last moment—I hope it will be that Mr. Paragon—will make us a little lopsided. Come down as soon as the first bell rings, and you will find me waiting for you—and then you will not be flustered by the mob of people. And, lest I should forget it when the time comes, don't pass the kromeskies, nor the crême renversée, my dear, whatever you do, for they're perfection, though perhaps I ought not to say so." And with that farewell word of advice, and a reassuring smile, Mrs. Hodlin Barmby sailed majestically out of the room, like a frigate parting from her convoy.

The idea of sitting next but one to Mr. de Coucy fluttered Evy not a little; not because he was likely to make her an offer of marriage, though *that* was a little embarrassing, but because his relationship to Lord Dirleton made him first cousin once removed to her own dear Jack. Everything else sank into insignificance before that tremendous fact. If she could only get him to talk of Jack, without his suspecting her tender interest in the topic, how very nice that would be; and yet, if she blushed as she had done just now, how could he help suspecting?

Here was another knock at the door, and in came Uncle Angelo with a pill-box in his hand.

"Do you think it would excite general

observation, Evy," inquired he, " If I were to take one of these little pills between the courses?"

"Indeed, I do think it would, dear uncle," answered Evy, appealingly.

"Very good, my dear; then I suppose I must be content with my Vichy water, and the elixir after dinner, for nobody will know that from sherry unless by the smell."

Here the first dinner-bell sounded, and Evy laid her small hand, which trembled not a little, on her uncle's arm, and descended to the salle-à-manger.

CHAPTER VIII.

IN WHICH MR. ANGELO HULET IS "UPSET.'

THE public dinner at Lucullus Mansion was a very different affair from English tables d'hôte in general, where folks converse in cliques, and glare at their vis-à-vis, or, silent as fishes, preserve a severe, but sad decorum, befitting a Cæsar when making his arrangements for perishing decently. After the company was seated, each person was here introduced to his or her neighbour, by either the master or the mistress of the ceremonies, and the character of an ordinary dinner-party was imparted to the affair as much as possible. Mr. Hodlin Barmby, a broad-shouldered "acred" looking gentleman, did the honours at the bottom of the table, and looked the genial host to perfection; he was not eloquent—unless you got him on a horse—but was always ready to come to the rescue of the conversation with the weather and the crops; and if it needed a dead lift, had only to look towards his better half, in a concerted manner, for the required assistance. He had his orders to refer to "my father, Sir Hesketh," when any new comer was present, but in other respects was very wisely permitted to take his own line; if any exceptional people were at table—whom a reference to the prospects for the next Derby was likely to shock—Mrs. Barmby took care to place them in her own neighbourhood. Under these circumstances the host had generally the pick of the company about him, while the hostess was surrounded with the feebler sort, who required colloquial manipulation.

On the present occasion, however, there were none of what Mrs. Barmby was wont to term her "delicate cases" at table, to whom the "doctrine" preached from the Balcombe pulpit was even more attractive than its "aspects;" and only one pair of "lay figures"—a banker from the City, reputed to be worth half a million, and his wife, who was said to have money of her own in the concern, and who maintained a financially phlegmatic air upon the strength of it. These sat on Mrs. Barmby's right, and next to them Mr. Paragon, an Australian colonist, who had come to England to spend in horseflesh what he had amassed by sheep, and who would have given his horseshoe scarf-pin to have been sitting beside Mr. Barmby, instead of between prim Mrs. Bullion and Mrs. General Storks, of the United States army, who made up for the silence of her other neighbour by a constant stream of inquiries concerning the progress of civilization in the Antipodes, to which he was very far from being in a position, either from personal experience or otherwise, to reply.

Mrs. General Storks was a rich widow, by no means without good looks, and though, as Mr. Barmby characteristically observed, "her voice was a little high up, and her dress a little low down, had her heart in the right place," as, perhaps, we may have some opportunities of observing for ourselves. On Mrs. Barmby's left was Mr. Hulet, who had himself placed his niece upon his other hand, in order, as he said, not to destroy the symmetry of the table by putting two ladies together; but also as I shrewdly suspect, with a view to taking his dinner medicines with the greater secrecy; for Mrs. Barmby, he reasoned, would naturally endeavour to screen the peculiarities of a guest from observation, while a male stranger might sniff at the elixir, and ask what on earth it was. So, after all, Evy found herself next to Mr. De Coucy.

He was a man of at least three score, but still handsome and upright, and though dressed in sober black, like a clergyman, had an unmistakably soldier-like appearance; indeed, in his youth he had served, and not without distinction, in the Austrian army, which he had quitted upon the demise of a relative who had left him a considerable fortune; his manner and speech were courtly to excess, and on one thin white finger, which he had a habit of laying on his cheek, in order, perhaps, to attract public attention, glittered an emerald gem of about two thousand years old, which he prized as Lord John Russell prizes the old Reform Bill, or Garibaldi his plighted word.

"You are looking at my ring," he would say, if his neighbour omitted to take any notice of it, "and, indeed, it is somewhat worthy of your attention." And then he would go on to state, at considerable length, how it had been engraved by Pyrgoteles for Alexander.

Beyond him sat Mrs. Sophia Mercer, a washed-out but lady-like looking personage, evidently come to Balcombe for the "aspects," and Miss Judith Mercer, a girl of eighteen—a little gipsy of great beauty, and with no more resemblance to her aunt than a carnation has to a daffodil.

"What a very beautiful girl you have for your neighbour," whispered Evy, with reference to this young lady, after the ice had been broken between Mr. De Coucy and herself, by a little talk about Balcombe.

"It is certain you can afford to say so, Miss Carthew," returned the old gentleman, gallantly; "but do you really think her good-looking? I have got into quite a hornet's nest here for asserting as much."

The gay old Lothario forgot to add what was the fact (though, to do him justice, he bore her no malice on that account), that Miss Judith herself had stung him by a refusal of his hand and gem.

"I think her charming," said Eva, frankly; "is that her mam——"

Here Mrs. Eleanor Mercer, who, with her niece, had been engaged in conversation with some folks on the other side of them, leaned forward and looked round towards Evy; doubtless somebody had passed a similar admiring observation respecting the latter, to that which she herself had made upon Miss Judith, and the old lady was curious to behold the newly-arrived belle. She was very near-sighted, and had to adjust a pair of gold eye-glasses before making the desired reconnaissance, which gave Eva, on the other hand, an opportunity of observing her. A pale-faced, and rather freckled female, with dollish blue eyes, was Mrs. Eleanor, but she had a gentle and pleasant expression, too, which rayed out into downright admiration as she gazed on Eva's blush-tinged cheeks and down-drooped eyes.

"Heaven have mercy upon us," gasped Mr. Hulet, softly.

"What is the matter, uncle?" inquired Evy, in alarm, for that gentleman had fallen back in his chair, with a scarlet countenance, and was pressing his hand to his heart.

"One of my spasms, dear, that's all; don't take any notice," replied Mr. Hulet, in a hurried whisper. "What a mercy it was that I brought my elixir." Then there was a faint pop of a cork under the table, and an odour, unhappily not so faint, began to pervade his neighbourhood, as though a chemist's shop had been suddenly opened.

"No, that is not Miss Judith's mamma," returned Mr. De Coucy, in answer to Evy's unfinished inquiry; "it's her aunt, and they are the very antipodes of one another. The one is, so to speak, faded and washed out, while the other is a very fast colour. How demure is the elder lady, how audacious the younger. A herald would call one a pelican in her piety, and the other a peacock in his pride—affronté you know—but perhaps you have not studied heraldry."

"No, indeed," answered Evy, a little distracted with anxiety upon her uncle's account; "it always seems to me very foolish."

"Foolish! Heraldry foolish! My dear

young lady!" And Mr. De Coucy held both his hands up (palm inwards, so as to keep the gem before the Public Eye), and threw his head back, as though somebody had clapped an ice-bag to his spine.

"My uncle always says there's nothing in it," explained Evy, apologetically; "he defines a crest to be 'a couple of jackasses fighting for a piece of gilt gingerbread,' and declares all the mottoes are made by the pastrycooks."

"My dear young lady," continued Mr. De Coucy, repeating that form of address with considerable unction, for it was his ingenious plan, when bent on conquest, to use his years as a stalking-horse; the "young lady" was first made accustomed to his paternally affectionate manner, and then on that agreeable foundation he made his approaches as a lover. "My dear young lady, your uncle deserves to be erased, as the king-at-arms would call it—cut off from society with a jagged edge; but it is terrible to think that an innocent"—he was going to say "angel," but he durst not—" young creature like yourself should grow up in such a damnable—don't be shocked, I take the expression from the thirty-nine articles — such a damnable heresy. If you would do me the honour of being my pupil for half an hour per diem for the next fortnight, I would answer for bringing you round to a very different opinion. As for heraldry being a useless science, nothing can be a greater mistake. Take up that spoon for instance, and tell me what you see in it? No, no, not in the bowl, for that would only show you a caricature of beauty, but in the handle."

"I see a stag walking," said Evy, quite unable to avoid a smile at the old gentleman's compliment, which was accompanied by a little bow in case it should have escaped her attention."

"Nay, pardon me, a stag is never walking in heraldry, but trippant. Moreover, it is not a stag but an antelope."

"But antelopes have not got double tails, and a tusk at the top of their nose?" said Evy, slily.

"Yes, they have—in heraldry. Now I should know that that was Barmby's spoon if I met with it in Otaheite. The cognizance has its origin in a circumstance that occurred in the family about 1480, and which is hereby commemorated by a sort of quaint pun, much affected in the heraldry of that period. Sir Gerald Barmby's *aunt eloped* when a young widow with Edward the Fourth (you remember how weak he was with respect to widows), by whose royal favour he became subsequently raised——"

"I beg your pardon," interrupted Evy,

gently, "but I think the ladies are going." And, indeed, that stiffening and rustling of silk were very audible, which betoken the preening of the female wing for flight.

"You are coming to the ladies' drawing-room, I hope, Miss Carthew," said Mrs. Barmby, pleadingly, as she rose from her chair.

"Thank you," replied she, with a hesitating look towards her uncle, "I don't think I will to-day."

"Yes, yes, go by all means," said Mr. Hulet, hurriedly. "It is well you should begin to make acquaintances. I will join you when I have finished my—hem"—he tapped his little bottle of elixir—"my Madeira."

This was one of the most powerful restoratives in her uncle's medicine list, and she had never known him take more than a single dose of it before, save once, upon the occasion of Lord Dirleton's visit. What could have happened to have upset him to such an extent that he was about to drink a bottle?

CHAPTER IX.

IN THE LADIES' DRAWING-ROOM.

THE ladies' drawing-room at Lucullus Mansion, though a large and handsome apartment, had not that stiff and formal air which belongs to its congener at a fashionable hotel. It was intended not only for show but for use, and thanks to Mrs. Hodlin Barmby's tact, even more than to the books and photographs, the besique boxes and chessboards, the comfortable ottomans and sofas, with which she had provided it, it *was* used. A hostess may provide conversation chairs, but cannot make her company talk—especially if it is a mixed one, and mostly strangers to one another—without some address; no, nor even sit in them, or else we should not find so many public drawing-rooms not only silent but empty.

At most hotels in England those who have private sitting-rooms prefer to make use of them in place of joining the general company, and those who have not that expensive luxury, often endeavour, by their absence from the evening gathering, to persuade people that they have; but at Lucullus Mansion there were very few ladies who did not spend at least the period during which their lords were sipping their claret—and excellent wine it was—in the drawing-room, and to none did Mrs. Hodlin Barmby omit to say "something civil." Those whom she saw evidently getting on well together, she wisely left to themselves after a passing word of courtesy, but where she saw "a hitch" she sat down, and smoothed the knot away, and set the skein going. More especially did she give her attention to the new-comers, whom it was her mission first to put at their ease, and then to introduce to such companions as she imagined would be to their taste. She brought her ducklings to the water, and set them swimming; and what mother duck could have done more?

On the present occasion, she naturally took Evy under her wing.

"Your uncle is somewhat of an invalid, I hear," said she, as they crossed the hall together in the rear of the cloud of muslin. "I noticed that he took Vichy water."

She must have also noticed that he had taken something very much worse; but to look at her when she spoke these words of sympathy you would have thought that she had had no nose.

"Yes, indeed, he is never very strong," said Evy, "but to-day he is unusually unwell, I think. I dare say the fatigues of our journey have been a little too much for him."

"Very likely, my dear. Else, being unaccustomed to him, I was rather frightened, do you know, to see him change colour so at dinner."

"Did you see that? I was in hopes nobody had observed him but myself."

"Well, nobody else did, dear, except you and me, I have no doubt," returned Mrs. Barmby, smiling; "but it is my duty, you know, to see everything—and to hold my tongue in most cases. I should have been careful of speaking of such a thing as this, for instance, to most young ladies in your position, but I did you the compliment of supposing you had common sense. It could not make your uncle any worse to mention the fact; while in case it had escaped your observation, it was only right to call your attention to it."

There was a certain seriousness in Mrs. Barmby's air that belied her careless words, and did not escape her companion's observation.

"You did quite right, I'm sure, and I am much obliged to you," replied Evy, gratefully. "To say the truth, I wanted my uncle to go upstairs at once, but he seemed to wish me to come into the drawing-room. It was not like one of his usual attacks at all. It seemed to me to be a sort of spasm."

"I think it was," said Mrs. Barmby; "but there is nothing to be alarmed at in that. They are common enough with all of us—I have them myself when anything puts me out—and especially with nervous subjects, such as I judge your uncle to be. You must tell me what is good for him, and he shall never be without a wholesome dish at table, I promise you."

"Oh, thank you. I have no doubt he

will do very well. He told me that the Balcombe air seemed to have done him good already."

"Indeed! Well that is very strange, for I understood him to say, not five minutes ago, that he was very doubtful whether it would suit him, and that I must not be surprised if he started off all in a hurry."

"Oh, you don't know my uncle," laughed Evy. "He threatened to leave Dunwich at least once a week, and yet we lived on there for three years."

Mrs. Barmby laughed with her young friend; but she did not share her apparently careless view of the matter.

"Mr. Hulet has got heart disease," was her private reflection, "and for half a minute at dinner to-day was, I am certain, in agony. It is just as well, however, that this poor girl should not be made aware of it—— Mrs. Storks, let me introduce my young friend, Miss Carthew."

"I am very pleased to make her acquaintance," said that lady, frankly, "and I wish, for both our sakes, it had been made earlier; I mean before dinner. I would then have talked to my vis-à-vis instead of my neighbour — oh dear, what a dreadful man that Mr. Paragon is, Mrs. Barmby—I flatter myself also that Miss Carthew would have got on with me better than with that heraldric old griffin, Mr. De Coucy."

"It is very ungrateful of you to say so, considering the terms in which Mr. De Coucy used to speak of you, Mrs. Storks," returned the hostess, smiling.

"Yes, used to," returned the widow, laughing heartily; "but now, I fear, I am no more in favour with him than is our fair friend yonder." She motioned with her hand to where Judith Mercer was sitting by her aunt's elbow with a huge photograph book between them; then added, as her hostess slipped away to make herself pleasant elsewhere, "Are you good at character-guessing, Miss Carthew? If so, do tell me what you think of that young lady."

"Well, I never saw a more beautiful face," began Evy.

"Or a better figure," put in Mrs. Storks, expanding her own very charming bust just as a swan does when scornfully contemplating another swan. "There can be no two opinions about her good looks. But are there not 'slumbering fires,' as the novelists say—'temper,' *I* call it—in those down-drooped eyes?—she knows we are talking of her at this instant, and therefore seems as meek as a dove—is there not impatience, too, in those taper fingers with which she is pointing out 'objects of interest' to that exacting old lady?"

"I did not know fingers were so significant," said Evy, smiling.

"What, don't you believe in chiromancy? Of course I don't mean the divination part of it, but in the indications that the hand affords. Well, at all events, you know what sort of tempers people have who bite their nails. That girl would bite her nails to the quick if it wasn't for spoiling the look of them. She is obliged to be all dutiful submission to her relative, who 'sits upon her' dreadfully; but she little knows she is sitting upon a volcano. Miss Judith will strangle that old lady some day, mark my words."

"Let us hope not," said Evy, a little shocked at the other's vigorous language, accompanied, though it was, with a smiling air.

"Well, I don't know about 'hoping not.' You have no idea how trying Mrs. Mercer is with her fainting fits (she has one a day) and her footstool, which is indispensable to her wherever she moves; it must be a dreadful thing to live with a hypochondriac. By-the-by, why does your uncle always take paregoric with his meals?"

"I did not know he did," said Evy, attempting a stiff manner, though very much inclined to laugh.

"But it was paregoric, wasn't it?" returned his unabashed companion. "Well, at all events it smelt very like it. I hope he doesn't worry you as Mrs. Mercer worries her niece?"

"Indeed he doesn't, Mrs. Storks; my uncle is the kindest of men."

"Ah, that's very nice, and particularly as I see you mean it. Not like that girl yonder who will come up and thank you 'for your kind attention to her dear aunt' if you happen to thread her needle for her, and at the same time will wish you dead. He's very susceptible though, isn't he? Kind old gentlemen generally are."

"Susceptible? How do you mean?"

"Falls in love, like Mr. De Coucy, with every young woman he meets, does he not?"

"Oh dear no," said Evy, laughing, this time outright; she found it very hard to be angry with Mrs. General Storks, though some persons found it very easy. "I never knew him do anything of the sort."

"Did you not? Well, I may be wrong, but it struck me more than once at dinner that he gave a very peculiar glance towards Miss Judith Mercer. Tried to look at her unobserved (which he didn't, I'll answer for it); you know what I mean?"

"I can't say I do," returned Evy, frankly. "And I am quite sure that Uncle Angelo never——"

"Hush!" interrupted Mrs. Storks. "Here is Mrs. Barmby coming on an embassage from the malade imaginaire. If I am not mistaken, you are going to be introduced to her Transparency."

And indeed the mistress of the house here came over from Mrs. Mercer with a polite request from that lady that Evy would be so good as to grant her the great pleasure of an introduction.

"A very well-meaning person indeed, my dear," whispered Mrs. Barmby, as she escorted her young friend across the room, "but a little peculiar."

"How good of you, I'm sure," lisped Mrs. Mercer, when the formality had been accomplished, though not with complete success in Evy's case, as soon appeared. "I would have come over to you, Miss Hartopp, if it were not for my legs, which Doctor Carambole says I am not to venture upon for at least an hour after dinner. Judith—this is my niece Judith; you are just about of an age, and must, I insist upon it, be great friends—go and take Miss Hartopp's place on yonder sofa, and let her sit by me awhile."

Judith, who had risen at Evy's approach, and saluted her with a courtsey so low that it almost suggested a mock humility, bowed her head, and instantly obeyed her aunt's behest, not however without shooting one lightning glance of jealous disfavour at the new comer. The next moment Mrs. Storks and herself were engaged in such animated conversation as is rarely carried on between two ladies, unless they have a very violent antipathy to one another.

"I hope you don't think it a liberty," commenced Mrs. Mercer, "that I should have asked Mrs. Barmby to play the ambassador for me; but the fact is I was so struck by a resemblance in your face—only you are prettier than ever *she* was—to a connection of my own, that I felt irresistibly drawn towards you. Would you mind just pushing my footstool about two inches, or say an inch and a half? Thank you — that's just right. Judith herself couldn't have done it better. What a contrast, by-the-by, you and my niece afford. The Rose of Sharon and the Lily of what's the name of the place? My memory is utterly useless; as for names, my dear Miss Hartopp, they go in at one ear and out of the other, though after all that is of no great consequence, for as Somebody very rightly observes, 'What *is* in a name?'"

Evy bowed adhesion: if Mrs. Mercer did not care about accuracy in names, why should she trouble her with the fact that her own name was not Hartopp.

"One often forgets names and dates," remarked she, wishing to say something comforting, "though one remembers other things well enough."

"Yes, but I don't remember other things, child," answered Mrs. Mercer, peevishly; "and when you get to my age, especially if you have had bad health—there, I've lost my knitting-needle. You don't happen to be sitting upon it, do you? Doctor Carambole knew a poor girl who did that once—no, by-the-by, she swallowed a packet of them, or perhaps it was only two of them, but at all events they increased and multiplied in quite a remarkable manner, and shot about all over her, and came out at her joints, her elbow joints particularly. You've found it on the floor. How good of you. Where was I?"

"You were speaking of the poor young lady who swallowed the needles."

"Just so; she wasn't a young lady, by-the-by, being only a milliner, but of course the principle is the same. Persons in her own rank who chanced to shake hands with her, used to have their fingers pricked most dreadfully. However, they cured her at last by mesmerism. They got a mesmer—no, I'm wrong, it was magnetism —they got a magnet, one of the things you buy at the toy-shops with metal fishes, you know, only larger, and all the needles leapt out at once, like a shower of rain. Talking of showers, are you going to stay at Balcombe long? You'll find it dreadfully wet."

"I cannot say; that will depend upon how it agrees with my uncle, who is an invalid."

"Dear me. Well, now, that's very nice —very interesting, I mean, of course. I wonder whether his symptoms are like mine. Would you mind describing them?"

"I believe my uncle's ailment is chiefly connected with the nerves," remarked Evy, evasively.

"Ah, then he will derive no benefit from being here, nor anywhere else. My dear Miss Hartopp, I've been everywhere for nerves, and never lost them, though I have acquired several new diseases. Balcombe is neither better nor worse for me than other places."

"You find it pleasant, however, do you not? The scenery seems exceedingly picturesque."

"I believe it is; but I am too near-sighted to see scenery. I am obliged to look at everything through these double glasses, which is very fatiguing to a person in my delicate state of health. I can't hold them up for more than half a minute at a time. Doctor Carambole says, 'Let your niece hold them up for you, then,' but that looks so ridiculous, you know. Most near-sighted persons have some natural advantage in this respect. Gentlemen, you may have remarked, who use a glass have got a bit of fat in the corner of their right eyes to hold it up with, and ladies who wear these double things have often a little knob on the bridge of their nose; but my knob—"

and here Mrs. Sophia Mercer ran her finger along her own nose, which was retroussée—" is at the very end of it, you see, and quite useless. How old are you?"

The abruptness of this inquiry was accompanied by no change of tone; gentle regret at the shape of her most prominent feature gave place to tepid interest in her companion's age, and that was all.

"I am eighteen," said Evy.

"I should have thought you younger. Now Judith, who is one-and-twenty, looks fully her years. Blondes and brunettes are so different in that respect. You will keep your youth for a certain time, my dear Miss Hartopp, and then fall suddenly—just as I did—all to pieces."

"I hope not," said Evy, laughing; "and, indeed, Mrs. Mercer, I don't see that you have done so."

"It is very good of you to say so, I'm sure, my dear; but I am a wreck. Sitting as I am now, with a footstool nicely adjusted—by-the-by, could you put it just half an inch nearer? thanks—and with a hard cushion—soft ones are worse than nothing—to support the small of my back, I present a tolerable appearance. But you should see me when I am getting up in the morning—I wish you would some day, for it's a long business, and I should like to have somebody to talk to besides Judith. That's what I admire so much in reading of the French kings. They received society in their bedrooms. I dare say you have read all about their great levées and their little levées, and so on, while their wigs were being curled, though there is nothing of that kind, thank goodness, about me. It's all my own hair, such as it is. You would never guess it to have been once a beautiful brown, just like your own, and so long that I could sit upon it. Can you sit upon yours?"

"Well, really," laughed Evy, "I never tried."

"Did you not? I could just do it by throwing my head back as though I were taking a pill. By-the-by, it must be nearly time for me to take one now; but there, Judith never forgets to remind me to the moment. She has such a good head. I dare say you look after your uncle in the same way. You must introduce me to him presently, for I am sure we shall have many topics in common. Who is that gentleman coming into the room? I can't find my glasses. Doctor Carambole says—God bless my soul and body!"

"Miss Mercer, your aunt is ill," cried Evy, terrified by the sudden change in her companion's appearance, even more than by her ejaculation. To sink back in her chair was an impossibility for Mrs. Mercer, because of the supplemental cushion, but her colourless face had turned to a livid white, and was drooping, with shut eyes, upon one side, in a very alarming manner. Before Evy had finished her sentence, Judith had crossed the room, and snatching up a bottle of smelling-salts that lay on the table, applied it to her relative's nostrils.

"Good heavens! what is the matter?" shrieked a chorus of female voices.

"It is a fainting fit," observed Mrs. Storks, quietly, more with the object of reassuring the trembling Evy, than of allaying the general anxiety.

"It is not," answered Judith, decisively, "or at least it is not one of those to which my aunt is subject."

One good soul ran for water, another kindled a wax light, and seized a quill feather, and Mrs. Hodlin Barmby threw wide the glass door, that opened on the garden terrace, to give the patient air.

Even these sovereign remedies failed of

their effect for several minutes, at the expiration of which Mrs. Sophia Mercer opened her eyes, and glanced around her in an apprehensive manner, while at the same time the colour rushed to her cheeks.

"The gentlemen are all gone, my dear," observed Mrs. Barmby, rightly translating the poor lady's look of distress. "You feel better now, don't you?"

"Yes, Mrs. Barmby, thank you; there's nothing, as Doctor Carambole says, like salts"—here the patient sniffed at it vigorously—"except senna. Who is it that is holding my head?"

"It is Miss Carthew," said Mrs. Barmby.

"Ah," sighed Mrs. Mercer. "Why did you tell me her name was Hartopp? Now I understand it all."

A remark containing an enigma so pregnant and profound that its solution must not be disclosed until our next chapter, and perhaps not even then.

CHAPTER X.

JUDITH'S LITTLE SUGGESTION.

"MY dear Miss Carthew," observed Mrs. General Storks, as they were taking a little stroll on the terrace together, on the third evening after Mrs. Mercer's "seizure"—for everybody was agreed it was not one of her ordinary "goings off"—"does it not strike you that there is a something growing up between your uncle and that hypochondriacal old maid?"

"What, Mrs. Mercer?"

"Mrs. Fiddlestick. She used to be very particular in calling herself Mrs.

Sophia Mercer before Mr. Hulet came. She is an old maid, of course, though she would very much like, if I am not mistaken, to exchange her brevet for substantial rank."

"Indeed, Mrs. Storks, I think you are mistaken," said Evy, gravely. "She told me, herself, that she was nearly sixty years of age."

"What has that to do with it?—

"'There swims no goose so gray but soon or late,
She finds some foolish gander for her mate.'

Or, at all events, she is always looking for one. I tell you that woman has got her eye on Mr. Hulet. She follows him about wherever he goes."

"Follows him about!" echoed Evy, in grave astonishment.

"Yes—that is, I mean, with her eye. It is true she sometimes looks very lackadaisically at Mr. De Coucy, but that is when she has not her glasses on, and mistakes him for your uncle. Then they are always interchanging prescriptions with one another; a very funny way of making love, it is true, but the only one open to them. People of sixty can't talk of their hearts in a sentimental way, but they can discourse of them medically, you know, in a very interesting manner. 'I always have a little palpitation when you are near me, my dear Mr. Hulet, and then I find these drops *so* efficacious!'"

The imitation of poor Mrs. Mercer's faded tone and manner was so perfect, that notwithstanding Evy felt not a little annoyance at her companion's suggestion, and the more so, since the idea had also occurred to her own mind, she could not forbear to smile.

"Doctor Carambole says," continued Mrs. Storks, in mincing accents, "that the very worst thing for a nervous disorder is to live a solitary life."

"You are really too bad," Mrs. Storks; "I don't believe Mrs. Mercer ever said such a thing as that to my uncle," said Evy, confidently.

"She doesn't say it for herself, my dear; she makes Doctor Carambole say it for her. And my own opinion is that 'no sich a person,' as Mrs. Betsy Prig said of Mrs. Harris, 'ever existed' as Doctor Carambole. That dyspeptic old lady merely quotes him as an authority for her indulging in anything unwholesome for which she has a mind; and she has a mind for Mr. Angelo Hulet. I don't mean to say your uncle is unwholesome," added the widow, precipitately, "but only unsuitable for her. It is not as if their complaints were different; for then they would get on with great success. But each of them is so 'shattered,' you see, and troubled with 'nerves,' that they would frighten one another to death."

"But I remember, Mrs. Storks, that you once accused my poor uncle of falling in love with Judith," reasoned Evy, whose mind was too fixed upon the main topic under discussion to take much notice of this direful prognostic.

"Very true, my dear; and I was correct in the fact, though wrong as to the person; I caught his eye, ranging with an expression it was impossible to mistake, towards the Mercers on the first day at dinner, and, of course, I concluded that he was smitten with that horrible girl. *That*, I allow, would be fifty times worse." And the widow shuddered as though she had inadvertently squashed a toad.

"Of course it would have been very— undesirable," answered Evy, rather at a loss for a word befitting such a catastrophe; "but I cannot see why you should entertain so great an aversion to Miss Mercer. I confess I did not like her myself at first, but I am beginning to have a much better opinion of her. Her devotion to her aunt is unquestionable, and—" Evy hesitated.

"And disinterested," put in Mrs. Storks, dryly.

"No, I was not going to say that," said Evy; "I was reflecting upon her conduct towards myself, which I think is singularly delicate, and even generous. If I were in Judith's place, and Mrs. Mercer had shown such especial goodwill to her, as she has to me, I am almost certain I should have been jealous. Now, on the contrary, the more I am in favour with her aunt, the more cordially Judith behaves towards me. I honestly tell you, dear Mrs. Storks, I think you are unjustly prejudiced against her."

"Perhaps I am; our styles are too much alike for us to be very good friends, you see," said the widow, naïvely; "whereas

you and she have nothing in common. I
don't mean to say that that ought to have
had anything to do with my aversion to
her," for Evy had opened her hazel eyes
very wide indeed, " though no doubt it did
lay the groundwork for it; nor do I assert
that if you had been a brunette instead of
a blonde, you would have been actuated by
my sentiments. I don't think you would.
You have the temper of an angel, and I'm
the other thing; I know that. But there
are degrees of blackness, and Judith is
several shades darker than I am, I mean
of course in character, for as to complexion,
she's a downright creole. She can't appreciate, for instance, a good girl as I can.
I am certain of it; and if she seems cordial
and friendly towards you—but here she
comes 'playing' her gold-fish as usual. If
her aunt marries, mark my words, she will
strike and land him."

The gold-fish was Mr. Paragon, who

along with Miss Judith Mercer had exchanged the drawing-room for the terrace for a little fresh air, and a flirtation. It was not often that he had such an opportunity; Judith was generally tied up to her aunt's side as tight as a marriage settlement, not from fear of her being made love to, but solely to push the footstool in exact gradations, and to hand the smelling-bottle at a crisis; but of late days, that exacting lady had dispensed with her niece's services after dinner, and Mr. Angelo Hulet had occupied her vacant chair.

"Confound it," murmured Mr. Paragon, "here's that North American Indian on the terrace."

His knowledge of geography was so limited that it may well have been that he thought he was correctly indicating a citizen of the United States by such a term, but on the other hand he had an intention to be depreciatory. He feared the tongue of Mrs. General Storks as the wild cattle of his native land fear the crack of the stock-whip. Nor could he trust Judith to defend him, as she was so well able to do. The widow and herself, if Lucullus Mansion had been an academy for young gentlemen, would have been in the position of those "cocks of the school" who though hating one another very cordially, are each averse to risk their supremacy in a decisive battle; and were certainly not likely to do so for the sake of Master Paragon. Moreover, had Judith taken up the cudgels for him, it would have been almost tantamount to acknowledging him as her lover, which she had not made up her mind to do. She suffered the slow, dull-witted youth to be bullied as he deserved, and even tormented him herself in public, though when alone together it is probable she patted him on the back. When he beheld Mrs. Storks and Evy, he knew that he would not be patted, and would probably be pinched, and hence his expression of annoyance.

"Mr. Paragon has just been making a proposal to me, ladies," began Judith in a sprightly tone.

"May we congratulate him?" interrupted the widow, "or have you made him wretched for ever?"

"Oh really," said Mr. Paragon, hurriedly, "you quite mistake."

He liked a flirtation very well, but he had by no means made up his mind to offer his hand to Judith. It was his boast that it had forty thousand sheep in it, and though Mrs. Storks had contemptuously designated it a "mutton fist," he knew its value.

"What a very rude man!" exclaimed that lady; "I hope he is not an example of colonial manners."

"Permit me to explain, madam," stammered Mr. Paragon; "my proposal includes yourself as well as Miss Mercer."

"Good gracious, that's not Australian, that's Asiatic;" cried the widow. "This is very shocking, sir, I must really inform Mrs. Barmby."

"I *have* informed her," persisted the unhappy Paragon, "and if you wouldn't take up a fellow so very sharp——"

"But are you so very sharp, Mr. Paragon?" inquired Judith, enraged at his want of gallantry to herself, exhibited, too, as it had been, in the presence of the enemy.

"Now don't, Miss Mercer, don't," pleaded the poor wretch; "why can't you tell her what I mean? The other men *would* make me their ambassador, because they said I was the youngest; but I knew I should make a mess of it. Look here, I am to make a proposal to all the ladies in the house, for all the gentlemen, you know——"

"Cupid's messenger!" observed Mrs. Storks, parenthetically.

"Well, I may be a stupid messenger, ma'am, but I defy Solomon himself to give a message if he was interrupted at every word. What I was commissioned to say, is—will you all accept an invitation to a picnic given by us to-morrow in Birbeck Woods? Miss Carthew—I know *you* will give me a civil answer at all events—what do you say? Will you deign to favour us with your company?"

Evy felt a sincere pity for this poor man, who, on hospitable thoughts intent, had been thus made a shuttlecock by her two companions for his pains, and she answered frankly that she would be very pleased to go to the picnic, if her uncle should approve thereof.

"Oh, he will certainly approve of it," said Mr. Paragon, "for he was the very one who suggested the idea. We are to have a lottery to settle the articles to be supplied by each of us, and the prize is to be the 'pepper and salt'—but there, I ought not to have told you about that."

"I should think you ought not," exclaimed Mrs. Storks. "And I only hope you may draw 'the wine' for your share. The idea of esteeming it an advantage to have to pay as little as possible for the benefit of us ladies. The 'pepper and salt' should have been your 'blank,' sir, if you had been a true knight."

"I am sorry I mentioned it," said Mr. Paragon, humbly; "but old Mr. Bullion called it 'the prize.'"

"I have no doubt he did," said Mrs. Storks, contemptuously; "and I dare say the risk he runs of having to pay for the champagne will keep him awake all night."

"Gad, you are right there," said Paragon eagerly, delighted to conciliate the widow, "and it shows how uncommon clever you must be to hit on that; for no sooner had the thing been agreed upon, when Bullion inquired of Barmby whether he did not think the champagne he gives us at dinner was not too good for a picnic; he meant too dear of course."

"Pray spare us these terrible details," cried the widow, laughing heartily, "or we shall not be prejudiced in favour of our hosts—and here they come." Under cover of her mirth, and of an irruption of gentlemen from the drawing-room to the terrace that here took place, Judith whispered a few words in Evy's ear and led her down the steps into the garden.

"I want to have a little private talk with you, Miss Carthew, if you will be so good as to give me five minutes."

"As many as you please, Miss Mercer," said Evy, kindly.

"Yes, your time is your own," answered Judith, with a bitterness that she seemed unable to restrain, "whereas I am accountable to another for every minute. However, it is not to bore you with my miseries that I have brought you here; my aunt says she likes all her friends to be prosperous, and it is true she does so; not so much from benevolence, I suspect, as because those who are rich and independent are not troublesome to her."

"I cannot think so ill of Mrs. Mercer as that," said Evy; "she is exacting it is true, and somewhat thoughtless of others, but I think she has a kind heart, and I am quite sure that she has a sincere affection for yourself."

"If so, she has a strange way of showing it," replied Judith, coldly. "But let that pass. It is not in human nature to expect one in your position to sympathize with a mere hanger-on like me."

"My dear Miss Mercer," said Evy, quietly, "you are not paying human nature a compliment. I flatter myself that if I was an heiress, as rich as Mrs. Bullion is said to have been, I should sympathize with you all the same, but as a matter of fact, I am just as dependent as yourself."

"Indeed! Is that so?" returned Judith, with interest.

"Yes; I have nothing of my own; whatever I have is given to me by my uncle, and yet I do not consider myself 'a hanger-on,' as you call it. He is generosity itself, and would be dreadfully distressed if he thought I entertained such an idea. The benefits of a blood relation are not like those of a stranger—and even in that case where there is a genuine mutual affection, there need be no distressing sense of obligation. As for your position, it seems to me, to be exactly similar to my own."

"No it is not. It is very different,

Miss Carthew." She hesitated, then added, "I know I can trust you to keep what is to me a most important secret. Mrs. Mercer is not my aunt."

"Not your aunt!"

"Hush! there are people on the terrace above us. No; she is no relation to me whatever. I was an orphan, and she adopted me. Suppose your uncle should take a fancy to a pauper child in Balcombe workhouse, and offer to relieve the guardians of all charge of it—well, that was my case."

Evy's astonishment was excessive, but so soon as she recovered from it, her first thought was how to show tenderness and sympathy for one who had thus made a confession which it was only too evident from her bitter tones, was humiliating to an extreme degree.

"Let me say one thing, Judith (if you will let me call you so), in Mrs. Mercer's favour," said Evy, gently passing her arm through that of her companion; "I should never have guessed from her manner to you that you two were anything less to one another than you are supposed to be. As for your secret, it is, of course, as safe with me as though you had never revealed it, and I cannot but feel gratified at the trust you have reposed in me. You had probably, however, some object beside that of merely showing confidence—nay, do not misunderstand me"—for Judith's face suddenly became scarlet. "I meant to say I hoped you had, since if I can further it, you may be sure that I will do my best to do so. I was an orphan, Judith, and almost a pauper myself, when Uncle Angelo adopted *me*." Evy's eyes were full of tears, and her voice trembled with tenderness, as she added, "Tell me—what can I do for you?"

"You are very kind, Miss Carthew,"

began Judith, in low but unfaltering tones——

"Please to call me Evy; that is the name to which I am most accustomed, and it sounds more friendly," interrupted Evy, gently.

"You are very kind, Evy. Much more so than I had any right to expect; and it is a comfort to me, finding you so, that my intended communication with you is not wholly a selfish one. The matter about which I wished to speak concerns us both, although not in the same degree. I wished to put you on your guard against Mrs. Mercer. She has a fixed design to marry your uncle."

"Do you really think so?" asked Evy, coldly. Not because she had any doubt upon the point, of which Judith's observation coming upon the back of her own and Mrs. Stork's suspicions made her only too well-assured; but in order, if possible, to discourage her companion from pursuing the topic. She had been quite sincere in her expressions of sympathy for Judith, but she did not like her as she did the widow, and even with the latter she would willingly have avoided a discussion upon her uncle's affairs.

"I am positively certain of it," answered Judith. "And when my aunt, as she calls herself, sets her mind upon anything, great or small, no considerations of propriety or convenience, prevent her from going through with it. She has been advised, for instance, to use spectacles, but though she is as blind as a bat, and would be taking the wrong medicines half a dozen times a day, if it were not for me, she will not wear them, and excuses herself upon the ground that she can't keep them on her nose. She has twice fallen downstairs in consequence of persisting in this folly, but she would rather break her neck than bend her will. Her will is now to marry your uncle in spite of public opinion; you may say, indeed, that in this case, there is another's will to be consulted, but Mr. Hulet, if you will pardon me for saying so, is weak and easily led."

Evy shook her head.

"I mean in this particular matter," explained Judith. "It is quite possible that he may be as obstinate as my aunt, when there is no occasion for it. Indeed, I heard him discussing the character of Charles the First yesterday with Mr. De Coucy, in a manner that convinced me that he is so. But there are few men who can withstand a woman's persistent attentions, especially when they are paid by one who is in the habit of exacting them from all the rest of the world. Besides, she has a great advantage to start with in their previous acquaintance."

"You think, then, that they have known

one another before?" said Evy, interested in spite of herself.

"Of course. I am convinced of it, and took it for granted that you were aware under what circumstances it happened. Is it possible that you know nothing of this?"

"Nothing; though I don't deny that the idea has suggested itself."

"Suggested itself!" echoed Judith; "when a lady faints away at the sight of a gentleman's face, it must be either a very forbidding one indeed—which is certainly not the case in this instance—or be connected with some association of the past. It was at the precise moment of Mr. Hulet's entrance into the drawing-room, if you remember, that Mrs. Mercer had her 'seizure,' as they call it."

"I was too frightened to notice that," said Evy, and indeed she thought it strange that Judith herself should have had eyes for aught else than the catastrophe that had happened to her aunt. Yet she was doubtless right. The emotion which Mr. Hulet had exhibited at the table d'hôte, of which however she did not now think it necessary to speak, joined to his subsequent behaviour—his long silences apparently spent in reflection, his unwonted references to the past (her past), and above all his reticence upon the subject of Mrs. Mercer, to whom he had at once attached himself as to an old acquaintance—had already now and again suggested to Evy that her uncle and Judith's aunt had met of old and been on a familiar footing, and now viewing it by the stronger light cast by Judith's intelligence, she was convinced of the fact. Still, she did not feel drawn towards her informant, as generally happens in such cases, or inclined to reward her sagacity with confidences. "I was too frightened to notice that," reiterated she; "but it is quite possible you may be right in your surmise."

"You take it very coolly, Miss Carthew," said Judith, scanning her quiet face with impatient eyes, "but it surely concerns us both that this ridiculous 'love affair,' if one can call it so, should if possible be put a stop to. Were you the heiress I supposed you to be, I should request your assistance upon general grounds; those of common sense, and good taste, for instance, both of which would surely be violated by such a match as this. I should have appealed to your regard for your uncle, who would be made a laughing-stock were he to commit such an act of folly as to marry this woman. The united ages of such a bride and bridegroom would be quoted in the comic newspapers. But situated as it seems you are, this matter becomes of the utmost importance —concerns yourself indeed almost as much as it does me."

"To tell you the truth, my dear Miss Mercer," returned Evy, gravely, "I do not see how it concerns either of us."

"Then you must be very dull or—no, I don't mean that—you must be singularly indifferent, my dear Miss Carthew, to your own interests. Being dependent on your uncle, is it of no consequence to you, do you imagine, that he should fall into the net of this designing woman? Are you aware that marriage invalidates a man's will, and that even if he be persuaded to make a second—itself often a difficult task—he will of course have another's interest to consult as well as, perhaps in place of, your own."

"Indeed, Miss Mercer," said Evy, colouring, "I have never given my consideration to such matters. They have not indeed so much as occurred to me; but since you have suggested them, I must confess they will cause me to be more careful, even than I should have otherwise felt it my duty to be, to abstain from the least interference with my uncle's proceedings. Do not imagine that I am blaming you, Miss Mercer," added Evy, perceiving her companion to droop her eyes as if in confusion, " or arrogating to myself an extraordinary delicacy. It is only natural that you should feel anxiety respecting the provision for your future; whereas in my case, I have such confidence in my uncle's generosity and affection, that I can feel no apprehensions as to any change he may think proper to make in the future distribution of his property."

"You are fortunate, Miss Carthew," sighed Judith, "and I am sure you deserve to be so. It is not every one who is so trustful as yourself, or so delicate where your own interests are concerned. Still, I will not have you imagine that I am so altogether sordid and selfish as my words, I fear, have led you to imagine."

"My dear Miss Mercer, pray believe me—" began Evy, in great distress.

"Yes, yes, I know you meant nothing harsh," interrupted Judith; "and it is most kind of you, I am sure, to feel the inclination to apologize to me. But let me say, in the strictest confidence, that I was not pleading for myself alone. You will not let it go further; you will not tell that odious woman, who is watching us from the terrace even now, and who would only jeer at such a confession; but there is one whose interests are bound up in mine—he is very poor, though he works very hard; a struggling artist——"

"Your brother?" said Evy, tenderly.

"No, Miss Carthew." Judith's voice sank to a whisper, and she cast her beautiful eyes upon the ground. "Some one even dearer than a brother. Oh, think if you were in my case" (if the speaker had looked up at that moment she would have had her secret reciprocated in her companion's blushing face and dewy eyes) "and felt your hopes of love—of this world's heaven—dependent upon a few pieces of gold, would not the vile dross itself acquire a certain sacredness in your sight, and excuse you for a prudence that otherwise, I own, seems so ill to befit my age and sex?"

"Indeed, indeed it would," said Evy, tenderly. "Forgive me if for a moment I misjudged you, Judith. My uncle must see this young painter, and——"

"Oh, pray don't speak of Augustus to Mr. Hulet," interposed Judith hastily; "my aunt detests the very mention of his name, poor fellow."

"Well, then, some other plan must be hit upon for the present, and as for the future, in case this marriage should take place, and if my influence can serve you with my uncle with respect to the provision that will doubtless be arranged for your future interests, rest assured it will be exerted to the utmost."

"Oh, thank you, thank you," answered Judith, her handkerchief held to her eyes to conceal her emotion, while her hand met that of her companion with a grateful pressure.

As for Evy, the thought of her beloved Jack separated from herself by disparity of fortune (though not, indeed, by the absence of it) even now, and possibly to be debarred from her for ever, melted her heart within her.

"I will do my best for this poor girl in her sad strait," thought she, "and Heaven help us both."

At the same moment, Mrs. General Storks, who, from her post of vantage on the terrace, had caught sight of Judith's handkerchief-hidden face, might have been heard to murmur to herself, "I wonder what piece of sentimental knavery that abominable girl is practising upon poor Evy." And when Mr. Paragon inquired at what object in the garden she was gazing so fixedly, she pushed that gentleman's credulity to its extreme limit by replying with gravity, " A crocodile."

CHAPTER XI.

THE RING AND THE RING GUARD.

THE invitation to the gentlemen's picnic was accepted (who ever knew it otherwise?) by the ladies of Lucullus Mansion with unanimous avidity, and late as it was, Mrs. Hodlin Barmby despatched emissaries that very night throughout Balcombe to furnish forth the sylvan board. That admirable woman never waited till the next day to secure what could be bespoken the same evening, and in that case, as in others, she had her reward; many a household in the neighbourhood went without its lobster and its lettuces on that eventful day, in order that the salad should not fail in Birbeck Beeches. She never gave way to that besetting weakness of her sex—a tendency to "risk" matters—and would rather bring home some coveted article of food, such as a pot of Devonshire cream, or a basket of plover's eggs, in her own hands, than put a respectable tradeswoman in the way of temptation of a higher bid. Nor was it only with the commissariat that she concerned herself. She marshalled the guests in such order as her sagacity foresaw would be most pleasing to them, and placed in each carriage—well horsed and gaily postillioned under her husband's eye—its due complement of passengers. It had got about that Mr. Angelo Hulet had been the proposer of the entertainment, and therefore the first vehicle was given to him, not a little to Mr. Bullion's indignation, whose vast possessions naturally inclined him to the belief that he had a divine right in everything over everybody. It was necessary to tell him, in order to appease his wrath, that Mr. Hulet (who was five years his junior) had had the pas of the rest of the company as being obviously the eldest. With the latter, of course, went Evy, and "since the young people would naturally like to be together," said sly Mrs. Barmby to the valetudinarian, "I shall send Miss Judith, and her aunt, along with you two."

The effect of this arrangement was to fill the pockets of the first carriage with so many bottles and phials, and packages of charcoal and digestive biscuits, that it might have been supposed by a casual spectator to be carrying the provisions for the picnic, which had in fact been despatched hours before, in a separate conveyance, to a certain appointed greenwood glade. The two invalids finding themselves thus in each other's company, and with every remedy and restorative at hand, and having nothing to complain of except their ailments—which was their favourite topic—looked eminently well pleased, and conversed with one another in low confidential tones. On the opposite side sat the girls; Judith, a little incommoded by the irrepressible footstool, but wreathed in smiles as in duty bound, while Evy, though she would rather have had Mrs. Storks beside her, looked equally happy if not quite so demonstrative.

"I can see that my spirits surprise you," whispered Judith to her companion, "and yet it is to you that I am indebted for them. Ah, you who are so happy little know what magic a few kind words, such as you spoke to me last night, can effect with one who is so unused to kindness. Perhaps you meant little by them," here she paused, and Evy answered quickly and earnestly :

"Indeed, dear Miss Mercer, I meant all I said."

"How can I believe that, when you will not call me Judith?" returned the other, pathetically. "Oh yes, I know it was an oversight, a slip of the tongue, and that you mean to be friendly with me, whenever you can think of it. It is not your fault, dear Miss Carthew. I have not, alas! the gift of attracting the love of others, as you have. Ah, how I covet it!"

"Indeed, Judith, you do me wrong," pleaded Evy; "and yourself wrong. I did not call you by your Christian name because of your aunt's presence, whose suspicions I thought might be aroused by such sudden familiarity."

Oh, Evy, Evy, when the recording angel had to write down that little speech, I am afraid it was not without some celestial hieroglyphic indicating a doubt of its authenticity. My own conviction is that you do not like your new friend so well, that terms of endearment for her spring, flower-like, on your lips—that you have in fact told "a white one."

"And as for your not attracting people," she continued, "I am sure the anxiety that Mr. Paragon, for one, showed to hand you to your seat just now, was a sufficient contradiction to such a statement. Don't you think it is a little hard upon the poor man to let him be so very civil in ignorance of the existence of—by-the-by, you never confided to me the name, which I hope to read of one day among the Royal Academicians."

"I dare not breathe it in this company," returned Judith, with emotion. "My vis-à-vis is not always so deaf as she was the other night, when she took Hartopp for Carthew. Yes, I am sorry for Mr. Paragon, but I don't think he is likely to break his heart about me or anybody else; and it is so necessary for dear Augustus's sake that I should dissemble. It was only the other night that my aunt was congratulating me upon what she was pleased to call my 'good sense,' in encouraging the attentions of one who could offer me an establishment instead of listening to 'a beggarly painter.' Was it not cruel of her, dear?"

"I think it was most abominable of her," said Evy, indignantly. "I should never have given her credit for such a speech, did I not hear it from your own mouth. With all her faults she seems so kind and lady-like——"

"My dear Evy," interrupted Judith' compassionately, "your charity leads you to be too credulous. Don't you see that my aunt has now a motive for appearing in her best colours, or rather in colours that don't belong to her at all? Only watch how she languishes when she addresses your uncle; whether she is talking of her love, or her liver, it's all one."

Evy could hardly forbear to smile, though she felt ashamed of doing so. Judith's conversation did not please her; it was clever, but too cynical, and even coarse, to suit her taste. Now Mrs. Storks was satirical and outspoken enough, but somehow, she was never vulgar; her geniality of disposition also enabled her to "say things" in a manner that robbed them of their sting, whereas the tone of Judith's talk (when she was not apologizing for it) was very hard. At the same time Evy was too just not to admit that the position of this poor girl put her at a great disadvantage; she had heard her uncle say that where dependence does not make a hypocrite, it makes a cynic, and had the lines of Judith's life fallen in more pleasant places, it was only reasonable to suppose that she would have been a more pleasant person.

Upon reaching their destination the hosts of the picnic proclaimed, as it were, their independence, threw off the yoke of Mrs. Hodlin Barmby, and rearranged the party in accordance with their own views. Each gentleman—so far as they went, for they were less numerous than their fair guests—carried off a lady, and escorted her to the glade where the collation was awaiting them, and as Birbeck Beeches, though but of small extent, was a pathless wilderness, there was no direct route, but every pair took their own way, which, in some cases, was an intentionally prolonged one. Those ladies on the contrary who had no cavalier, but were obliged to put up with a substitute (even though it was Mrs. Bullion, who in inches was almost a man, and who had also a very respectable moustache) went as straight to the feeding place as their knowledge of the locality would permit, and Birbeck Beeches was pretty well known to all Balcombe. It was a very beautiful spot, as wild as a primeval forest, though you could scarcely have been lost, or starved to death in it, even if you had not stumbled on the hampers from Lucullus Mansion—and every tree was "a study" for any young woman who could wield a pencil, and had advanced as far as a number three drawing-book. Each mighty bole was mossed and knobbed in some characteristic fashion, and with its gnarled branches presented in numberless instances a grotesque likeness to the human form. To Monsieur Gustave Doré's eyes, indeed, the wood would have been ready "peopled," even without the presence of the picnic party; and the sharp-tongued Judith pointed out so many sylvan likenesses of residents in Lucullus Mansion to her companion, Mr. Paragon, and that so wittily, that that gentleman, albeit not easily moved to mirth (of which he was always somewhat suspicious, lest he himself should be concerned in evoking it), had more than once to seat himself on the thick piled moss to have his laugh out; on which occasions Judith very good-naturedly sat down also. "If these little opportunities should occur after our champagne luncheon," was her sagacious reflection, "this man will propose to me to a dead certainty. And what shall I do then?"

Evy was under the sober convoy of Mr. De Coucy, who perceived, or pretended to perceive, in the trees, certain heraldic resemblances which enabled him to hold discourse upon his favourite topic, and to commence that course of instruction with which he had already menaced his fair companion. *He* also sat down on the moss, and pressed her to sit beside him, in order that he might more conveniently expatiate upon the alerion—a neighbouring wood-cut—which he was careful to observe, though modern heralds had degraded it into a monster, was indeed originally no other than our eagle, the cognizance of the House of Lorraine, and an anagram upon its name. When the unconscious tree had done its duty, he passed on to others, nor was he long before he found a beech likeness in profile to Alexander the Great, which gave him the wished-for opportunity of calling attention to his ring by Pyrgoteles; a subject that furnished him with the materials for so long a lecture that among the crowd of thoughts that flitted across Evy's mind during its progress, the reflection that it was lucky that the collation which was awaiting them could not get cold, found an involuntary place.

"What is that funny creature on that other ring of yours?" inquired Evy, presently, not that she cared, poor little soul, what it was, but that Pyrgoteles was wearing away the life within her, and any change of topic seemed acceptable; "I think I have seen something like it before."

"Funny creature! my dear young lady," replied Mr. De Coucy, in a tone that protested against such epithets, as not only inapplicable, but sacrilegious, "that is the tailless gryphon; I wear it on my signet-ring, as being the cognizance of the family to which I have the honour to be not distantly related; the Heytons."

"To be sure," said Evy, with an unexpected interest; "I remember to have seen it sculptured above the great gates leading into Dirleton Park at home."

"Ah, yes; since you have lived at Dunwich, you are doubtless acquainted with my noble relative."

"Very slightly; that is, I have only seen him once," said Evy.

"Well, he is not much to look at," observed Mr. De Coucy, smiling, "though he is a very excellent fellow when you come to know him; but you must have met his nephew, Captain Heyton—or as we call him, Jack."

"Yes; I have met Captain Heyton—three or four times," answered Evy, with a desperate effort to appear at once indifferent and exact.

"Well, isn't he a capital fellow? All the family except his cousin Dick, who is no more to be compared with him than that scarabæus,"—here Mr. De Coucy prodded his umbrella viciously at a wandering beetle,—"delight in Jack."

Evy blushed with pleasure—she had liked this old gentleman well enough, but had hitherto considered him a little tedious; now she confessed to herself that she had made a mistake, and that he had a very agreeable way of putting things.

"Captain Heyton was a general favourite in Dunwich, I think," assented Evy.

"So I should imagine," said Mr. De Coucy, "or his neighbours must be hard to please. Why to begin with, he is one of the best-looking fellows in England. Don't you think so?"

"He is certainly good-looking," said Evy, worrying the scarabæus in her turn with the tip of her parasol.

"Yes, indeed, and his face does not belie his heart. The old lord, between ourselves, would be unbearable if it was not for Jack's civilizing influence. I never go to the park myself unless Jack is there. His smile irradiates the old house like a perpetual sunbeam."

What a charming old man this was after all, and what a stream of pleasant talk lay in him, when that rubbish of alerions and gryphons did not choke it! Why didn't he go on? She looked up with a radiant face to know the cause of his sudden silence, and met his keen gray eyes gazing down upon her with curious earnestness.

"Captain Heyton is very much looked up to in our neighbourhood," remarked she, with as great presence of mind as she could assume; "he is the life and soul of the rifle corps, and—and—of the cricket club, and all that."

"I don't doubt it," replied Mr. De Coucy; "'noblesse oblige,' you know; it is—or ought to be—his place to take the lead in everything of that sort. He will be one day Lord Dirleton himself, and in all probability inherit his uncle's wealth as well as title. There is not a better match in the county I should say than Jack. He will probably marry some duke's daughter; indeed, I have heard his name associated with one already, though I forget who it was; perhaps you have happened to hear it."

"No," said Evy, as carelessly as she could. "I don't think I have."

What a dreadful old man this was after all, and how fond of scandal. Even Pyrgoteles was a preferable subject of conversation to that which he had now selected. If the wandering scarabæus had not by this time made a tunnel for himself into the moss he would probably have suffered death by impalement.

"Don't you think that they'll be waiting luncheon for us, Mr. De Coucy?" said Evy, after a long silence.

"No, my dear young lady, I don't think Mrs. Bullion would permit them to wait for anybody. You seem to have taken a fancy to this ring of mine; would you do me the favour to accept it?"

"Oh no, Mr. De Coucy," said Evy, recollecting, for the first time, Mrs. Barmby's warning with reference to her companion's weakness for making proposals of matrimony. "I could not think of doing that. I have heard you say yourself that the gem was two thousand years old, and of priceless value."

"Nay, I didn't mean that ring, Miss—Evy, not but that I would even part with that, on one condition. That is if you would consent to wear beside it——Don't be alarmed, my dear young lady," continued he, gravely, for he had taken hold of her hand, in a parental sort of way, it might be, but also, perhaps, with a less platonic intention, and she had withdrawn it rather abruptly—." I am not going to ask you to marry me, because I am afraid it would be out of the question; you needn't say so; I see it. It is the gryphon ring I wish you to accept in token of my—my"—the poor old gentleman gave a little sigh of regret which, notwithstanding her displeasure, touched Evy's tender heart—"in token of my most sincere friendship. It will be acceptable to you, I know, for I have read your secret—upon another's account at least, if not on mine. Keep it for my sake —or Jack's. If it reminds you when you look at it, of a certain hopeless adorer (which it may do from his likeness to a gryphon—not so?—well, thank you for that at all events), I shall be gratified; for as to Jack—happy dog—you will not need a reminder. What I have said, however, about his being a great match is true— though not about the duke's daughter, which I invented to resolve my suspicions —and I can foresee that the course of true love will run at least no smoother in your case, my dear young lady, than it usually does. Indeed, it must needs meet with greater obstacles than common. If Reginald de Coucy "—here he gallantly placed his hand upon his heart—" can aid at any time in removing them, or in performing any other friendly service for you, you may trust him to do so. The ring "—here he respectfully placed it on Evy's finger—" is twice as large as it should be; which is of the less consequence since even if it fitted you, you would not, probably, at present, care to wear it. I will have it taken in at the jeweller's, and then you will keep it, till the day, which I hope to see, when you may wear it as a guard above Jack's wedding-ring. An old man's blessing on your ring, dear, and "—he hesitated a moment, meditating, perhaps a paternal kiss on the forehead, then added cheerfully—" and now let us go to luncheon."

CHAPTER XII.

UNDER THE GREENWOOD TREE.

THE cold collation was all that could be expected of it, and much more than what could have been expected by those who had been used to picnics, but not to Mrs. Hodlin Barmby's superintendence of them. It was not necessary to place the champagne "within the cooling brook," because ice had been duly provided for that purpose by her forethought, nor was it incumbent upon the gentlemen to neglect their own wants to minister to those of their fair companions, since the staff of attendants was fully sufficient to "wait on appetite." Whether digestion did so or not is doubtful, since of chairs and table there were none (how those old Romans must have suffered, by-the-by, who eat their food leaning on their left elbows!) and twice or thrice did the contents of Mr. Bullion's plate, who had no lap (but only a sort of money bag), slide off his knees to fertilize the mossy lea. However, what was wanting in comfort was made up for by the charm of novelty and the beauty of the dining-hall, with its roof of cloudless blue showing through the green rafters that sprang from those pillars of silver beech. It was taken note of at the time, to be remarked upon afterwards with great significance, that Mr. Angelo Hulet forgot to take his usual dinner pill before sitting down to this exceptionally unwholesome repast, and that Mrs. Sophia Mercer, though seated upon a moss-grown stump considerably higher than her customary chair, omitted to inquire for her footstool.

When the meal had been discussed, and the whole party arose to wander in the wood, while the servants took their places, this dyspeptic pair gradually dropped behind the rest until they were quite alone. It was the first time they had been so since they had met at Lucullus Mansion, though they had contrived under cover of medicinal discussion to have many a confidential talk together, and the circumstances seemed not a little embarrassing to them both. At all events neither spoke until they came to a little pool, overhung by one giant beech, that stood a little apart from its companions, like a monarch attended by his court.

"Do you remember this spot, Sophia?" asked Mr. Hulet, with a tremor in his tone that on this occasion at least might without any affectation have been set down to nerves; "and — and — what happened here?"

"Could I ever forget it?" replied she in whispered accents. "I have never been here since, Angelo, yet I have pictured the place ten thousand times."

"And yet it was near forty years ago," sighed he. It was a very genuine sigh, and came from the bottom of his heart; for the moment he felt as deeply as any poet (the most unpractical of us do sometimes), how once in that very wood he had walked with one he loved nine-and-thirty years ago; and,

"In the silver beechwood where he walked that day,
  The nine-and-thirty years were a mist that rolled away."

"What is forty years," answered she, not plumbing the depths of his sad thoughts, but answering to the sentiment upon the surface, "what is forty years or four hundred to a woman who has once loved?"

"Did you know that this was the very day—the anniversary?" inquired he, touching gently the hand that rested on his arm.

"How can you ask me such a question, Angelo!" remonstrated she.

"I thought you might have forgotten the date, though not the fact. I had done so myself, but was reminded of it the other day, when looking over an old diary."

"Ah, we women need no diaries for such a purpose," answered she with a plaintive look—which was, however, a little hypocritical, since as a matter of fact, she had herself forgotten the date in question altogether until reminded of it by her companion. "Such dates are engraved on the tablets of our hearts."

"I wonder whether we shall find it on the tablet of this beech tree," returned Mr. Hulet dryly, advancing towards it, and examining carefully its mossy bole. "I remember cutting it out with my penknife, and our initials also—and see, dear, here they are."

About five feet from the ground, much overgrown with lichen, and almost healed by the slow cure of Time, could be still discerned certain gashes in the ancient trunk which might stand for A. H., S. M., with the date in question.

"In twenty years more there will not a trace be left of them," remarked Mr. Hulet; "though to be sure that will not affect us, Sophia, will it? We shall be effaced ourselves by that time."

"*I* shall, Angelo, without doubt," returned his companion despondently. "There is a something here—no, it's a little higher," (she took hold of Mr. Hulet's hand, and just as Sir Isaac Newton used his sweetheart's finger for a tobacco-stopper, applied it like a plaster to her fifth rib or thereabouts)—"can't you feel something beating? —that tells me I am not long for this world."

For a moment the claims of dyspepsia were paramount; but suddenly recollecting that the occasion was supreme, and Love its master, she added with downcast eyes, "But to be sure it is no wonder that my heart should beat, with one that was once so dear, so near to it—Angelo."

"But even that can't account for its beating on your right side instead of your left," answered her companion, peevishly. "If you really had heart disease as I have, you would never make a mistake of that sort, my good woman. By Jove!—it's coming on now—how I wish I had not left those invaluable drops in the pocket of the carriage!"

"Take *my* drops," said Mrs. Mercer eagerly, and proffering a little phial. "There is nothing," as Doctor Carambole says, "like an immediate application of a remedy, even if it be not the one most precisely adapted to the case. 'If your salts are not at hand,' he used to say in his funny way, 'take a swig at your sal volatile.' Do you feel better, Angy?—that is, I beg your pardon, Mr. Hulet—oh, say you feel a little better."

"Yes; I feel much better. And I don't mind your calling me Angelo (you know I never liked 'Angy') if you prefer it. I don't mean to pretend, Sophia, that I should have sought you out designedly, nor even perhaps should have come to Balcombe had I known you were there; but having found you——" here Mr. Hulet hesitated, and stroked his chest, whether to indicate affection, or to assist the action of the drops he had just swallowed, was not quite clear; Mrs. Mercer, however, took it for the former.

"It seems like a providence, Angelo,

does it not?" said she demurely, "that we two should have thus accidentally met together after a separation of forty years." Here she covered her eyes with her hand, though not without regarding her companion between her fingers, and exclaimed pathetically, "Oh why, oh why, did we ever part?"

"You can answer that question yourself better than I can do it for you," answered Mr. Hulet brusquely.

"Oh, Angelo, how can you say so!" pleaded his companion.

"Because it is necessary on an occasion of this sort, Sophia," returned he, "above all things to speak the truth. You and I are here, if I mistake not, for the purpose of coming to a mutual understanding—and —and—in hopes to dove-tail our present with our past; to bridge over the great gulf that has intervened since we last met; to make reconciliation, and so far as is possible, atonement with one another. This cannot be effected by false representations on either side; let us allow we were both in the wrong, and have done with it. Perhaps I was irritable and impatient——"

"No, no," remonstrated Mrs. Mercer softly. It was not the least like the "no, no," of the House of Commons, but rather that conjunction of negatives which British grammarians describe as making an affirmative; freely translated, it might have been rendered, "Well, you certainly were all that, but don't let us talk about it." It seemed that some few grains of the irritability and impatience referred to still lingered in Mr. Hulet's composition to judge by the tone in which he replied:

"Very good then; if I was not, it was certainly your fault—as, indeed, I always maintained it was. You worried me beyond bearing with your caprice and obstinacy, and especially with your depreciation of my respected ancestor."

Mrs. Mercer's mild blue eyes, which had hitherto been moist and tender in their expression as those of a sucking-pig, here suddenly became, as it were, hard boiled; and the smile upon her lip took an upward curl.

"It was very foolish of me, I allow, Angelo," said she, "to argue with you upon that matter."

"It was not only foolish, madam, but it was unbecoming, and in the worst possible taste. However, let that pass; I should not have alluded to it, if you had not made that idiotic inquiry, 'Why did we ever part?' It is my honest desire that we should forget the past, except so far as it may endear us to one another. I don't want to make a fool of myself at my time of life by talking sentiment, and any unnecessary emotions cannot fail to aggravate our respective symptoms, and be hurtful to us both; but I don't deny that I feel towards you, Sophia, as I little thought—when we parted years ago—ever again to feel. When I met you that day at the table-d'hôte, it seemed really—if it isn't a bull to say so—like falling in love at first sight for the second time. It put me in such a state that I took nearly a pint of paregoric."

"Did you indeed?" replied Mrs. Mercer, once more all smiles again. "Now that was very touching; and I am sure I wished for my part, when I first saw you enter the drawing-room, that I had had some paregoric to take. You cost me a terrible spasm, Angelo."

"So I understood," replied Mr. Hulet, with the air of a man who is flattered at the sensation he has produced; "and the emotion did you credit. Well, the effect in my case at least was not transient. I said to myself, 'Sophia may have had her faults—as indeed, my dear, you had—'but after all, what woman is perfect? Taught by experience, and improved by nine-and-thirty years of solitary reflection, she will doubtless be now another creature.' I found you so, Sophia, while in all that formally endeared you to me—ahem!—or nearly all—for, Gad, what a beautiful girl you were in those days——"

"Was I?" answered Mrs. Mercer, softly; "and ah, what a handsome fellow were you, dear Angy!"

"Well, yes," said her companion thoughtfully. "When we looked down into this very pool together as we are looking now, I suppose it did give rather a different reflection of the pair of us. But you are a very fine woman still, Sophia, upon my life you are."

The tone of the speaker was grave and genuine; that of one who imagines he is speaking the truth, even if it be not the truth; and it thrilled his companion's ancient frame with grateful tenderness, nay, almost re-kindled the cold embers on the hearth of love.

"You were always a gentleman, Angelo," rejoined she, humbly. "Incapable of an unkind word, unless provoked, and most sensitive with respect to the feelings of others."

"But, by Gad, I mean it, Sophia," continued Mr. Hulet, earnestly. "Some poet—I don't know who—speaks of some pretty girl—at least, I suppose it must have been that—who was a sight to make an old man young; well, when I first saw you at Balcombe, I swear, I felt like a young man again. 'If Sophia will forgive me,' thought I——"

"There was nothing to forgive, Angelo," whispered his companion.

"Oh yes, there was. I was a cantankerous brute enough, I have no doubt.

However, let me finish. I made up my mind, I say, from that moment to ask you to let bygones be bygones. I arranged this picnic for that very purpose, and fixed it upon the anniversary of a certain event, with this very identical pool and tree in my mind's eye. There must have been some sentiment left in me, you must allow, to have planned that, eh? and now it has all come to pass so favourably thus far, let me ask you to crown my little plot with success. Underneath this tree, where we first plighted troth, dear Sophy, let us once more renew it. Come, what say you, 'yes,' or 'no?'"

There was no need for her to reply to the question, for the answer was written in her face; its wrinkles had suddenly become smoothed away as if by magic, its look of feverish discontent about the mouth, which habitual ill health had engendered, was exchanged for a graceful smile; the downcast eyes were lifted up, and met his own with that sunny glance, which a hundred winters cannot so utterly kill, but that it melts their snows, and shines out once again upon some beloved object—though it be from the death-bed. Mr. Hulet bent down his face, and kissed her tenderly; it was the first kiss he had given to woman (save to his niece) since he had parted from this one, nearly two generations ago, and a sacred privacy one would have thought was due to it. The genius loci, however, being probably some satyrical character, had deemed otherwise; for scarcely had the salute been administered, and as tenderly reciprocated, when a half-suppressed shriek of laughter rang out through the wood.

"Oh my goodness, somebody has seen us, Angelo; who can it be? Pray give me back my drops," cried Mrs. Mercer, nervously.

"I don't care who has seen us," answered Mr. Hulet, boldly, "though I think I recognize in that idiotic yell, the tones of that fellow from the antipodes—Paragon. We must be prepared for the ridicule of fools, and hold ourselves above it. Take my arm, Sophia—the arm that you will lean on so long as I live—and let us rejoin our friends."

CHAPTER XIII.

EVY ASKS A FAVOUR.

THE picnic party came home at eve from Birbeck Beeches in the same order as they went, but by no means under the same circumstances. It was observed by the other occupants of their respective vehicles that Mr. De Coucy, who was commonly a great talker, and especially when ladies were present, maintained a complete silence; whereas Mr. Paragon, who was ordinarily as dumb as Memnon's statue (without its exceptional conduct in the early morning), was loquacious and restless. If Mr. Bullion's proposition of the cheap champagne, with which the colonist had so improperly made merry, had been carried, things might have happened otherwise; but as it was, exhilarated by the best and purest Perrier Jouet, he had proposed to Judith, and was certainly under the impression that he had been accepted. Judith, on her part, without confiding this tremendous event to Evy, was more affectionate and demonstrative to her than ever; and Mr. Hulet and Mrs. Mercer sat opposite to them without interchanging a syllable, but with their hands fast locked together beneath the railway rug. If the former had ever sat to a sculptor he might have been correctly, as well as poetically, rendered, with "gout flying about him," but it had never settled anywhere; and when, like a little mouse, Mrs. Mercer's tiny foot stole towards his own, and softly trod upon his toe, he smiled a welcome to it. Once or twice she made a mistake, and trod on Judith's, but that sagacious young woman, far from exposing the error, made the expected reciprocation with the utmost good nature. A more complete example of doing good, or at least of conferring happiness on another by stealth, it would be difficult among the Annals of Good Deeds to find.

When Evy put up her cheek for her uncle to kiss that night before retiring to her room, he pressed his lips to it with unusual kindness, but in place of opening the door for her as usual—for notwithstanding his invalidish ways, he was as polite as Chesterfield—he motioned her to a chair, and said,

"Don't go just yet, Evy, I want to talk with you."

She knew what was coming quite well, and would gladly have relieved him from his evident embarrassment by telling him so; but on the whole she judged it better to be silent.

"I am going to tell you something," he began, "which at the first blush will cause me, I fear, to sink in your good opinion, Evy—that is I mean"—for she had shaken her pretty head, and smiled a smile that was a thousand negatives—"as to my good sense and judgment. When an old fellow of sixty-five bethinks him of matrimony, folks are inclined to compliment his heart at the expense of his wits; and I think they are mostly right."

"That must depend on circumstances, uncle, surely."

"Just so. A lonely man far advanced on the down-hill of life may marry for company's sake, to insure a faithful friend to tend him at the last; but no such excuse could be given for me, who have the dearest and most dutiful of friends in you, Evy."

"You are very kind to say so, uncle,"

said Evy, the tears gathering in her beautiful eyes in spite of herself.

"I only say the truth, and less than the truth, my darling, and being so fortunate as I am in possessing such a niece, I allow that it would be the height of folly in a widower such as you have always supposed me (as I conclude) to contract anew a matrimonial alliance."

Here he stopped a little, and fell to pacing the room, while Evy sat in silent astonishment; she could not have helped him on to his explanation now, even if she would.

"The fact is, my darling, Mrs. Angelo Hulet" (he always called himself Angelo, though he was an only son) "is still alive, and under this very roof. Perhaps you can guess now, who it is?"

"It is Mrs. Mercer, I suppose, uncle?"

"Yes; it is Mrs. Mercer, or Mrs. Sophia Mercer, as she calls herself, since after our separation she reassumed her maiden name. We parted from one another, by mutual agreement, nearly forty years ago, upon the ground of incompatibility of temper, after a very short experience of one another indeed. It may be urged that people's tempers do not alter—except for the worse—with time, but I hope that we are both at all events a little wiser, and shall be able to act towards each other more judiciously. At all events we have made up our minds to try the experiment."

"I wish you joy, my dearest uncle, with all my heart," cried Evy, rising and throwing her arms about his neck. "If you were about to make a new alliance, I should certainly not have dreamt of questioning your judgment; but to return, even thus late, to one whom you have prom——" Here Evy coloured, recollecting that it was not her duty to preach to her uncle, and came to a full stop.

"Promised to cleave to until my life's end, you were about to say, Evy," said Mr. Hulet, rubbing his nose in comical embarrassment; "yes, I am quite aware of that fact; but the truth is (though it is not generally known) that the compilers of the marriage service were for the most part—bachelors. As to loving, that may be possible with persons of exceptionally good principle, for it is said one ought to love even one's enemies, but I defy a saint to 'cherish' a woman that won't be cherished. If, for example, when you offer me that arrowroot which you make so admirably, my dear Evy, I were always to knock over the basin with the back of my hand, you would give it up at last as a sheer waste of time and trouble. You would be a fool if you didn't. Well, that was my case, or something like it, with respect to Sophia. However, *de disjunctâ nil nisi bonum*, and especially when you are going to be re-united. She is as kind-hearted a woman as ever lived, notwithstanding her little foibles; and that which rocommends her to me as much as anything is, that she has taken a genuine liking to yourself, Evy."

"Mrs. Mercer has been always so demonstratively kind, uncle, that it is a real pleasure to me to find in her a near relation."

"And I have no doubt she will continue to be so, Evy. If I thought otherwise she should be no wife of mine again, I promise you. Indeed, I have considered your interests throughout this matter, as indeed it was my duty to do, fully as much as my own. In the first place, Evy, it is thoroughly understood between your aunt and myself that our reunion shall not in any degree affect your future position. Neither she nor I, to do us justice, are very covetous people; when we parted company on our life journey, as we thought for ever, each of us took the entire fortune which severally belonged to us without invoking the tender mercies of the law, and now that I have told her that you will not only be my heiress, but that I am resolved to settle an ample provision on you in the event of your marriage, so far from offering any objection, she seems inclined to increase your fortune out of her own funds."

"Indeed, indeed, uncle, I have deserved no such kindness, even at your hands," sobbed Evy, overcome with the old man's affectionate solicitude. "Oh, how can I ever thank you for it as I ought?"

"First, by drying your tears, my darling," returned Mr. Hulet, tenderly; "and then by telling me that you will not desert your old uncle, or cease to fill his house with sunshine, until such a time as Lord Dirleton's 'Jack'—if he is to be the fortunate man—or some other equally lucky dog, comes to take you off my hands. I may need you more than ever now, Evy, though I hope and believe I shall not, and on the other hand if all goes well, and your aunt and I prove a comfort to one another, you will have the satisfaction, when your wedding-day comes—and a very, very sad one to your selfish old uncle it will be, my dear—of knowing that you leave me, not as you would now, a lonely valetudinarian, dependent upon hireling aid for his many wants, but in good hands; such as understand making possets, and applying poultices, and every art that can make home happy; don't you see, my darling?"

She saw as well as her tears would let her. It was evident that the kind old gentleman was affecting for her sake a cheerfulness, and perhaps even a confidence, that he was very far from feeling.

"Well, well, that is settled, my dear," continued he. "Your aunt and I have no preliminaries to go through in the way of wooing, nor even of wedding, and shall be reunited almost at once. In the meantime and while I am still my own master—for one never knows what may happen; a man may hold his own at one time, as indeed I did, and pass under the yoke at another—is there anything you would like to ask of me? It would be a pleasure to me, as you know, to grant it."

"Indeed I have all I want, and more, dear uncle," said Evy. "But there is a favour which I would very earnestly entreat of you for another—for poor Judith. I don't think she is quite such a favourite with her aunt——"

"She is not her aunt; she is your aunt," observed Mr. Hulet.

"That may be, dear uncle, but up to the last week she has been in the position of her near relative, and certainly taught to believe that she would be provided for as such. Now, pleased as I am to have won Mrs. Mercer's affection, it would distress me very much if I thought I had done so at Judith's expense."

"I don't see how you can help being liked, Evy," returned Mr. Hulet, "nor even being liked better than Judith. It seems to me, though I have nothing to say against the young lady in question, that you are worth ten thousand of her."

"You may be just a little prejudiced in making that estimate, Uncle Angelo," said Evy, smiling. "But, at all events, it would make me very miserable should our respective interests come into collision with any disadvantage to Judith. What I have to entreat of you is to use your influence with my aunt in her favour; some suitable provision would, I suppose, in any case be made for her, and if, as you hint, Mrs. Mercer was so good as to think of adding to my fortune, I would greatly prefer that

that sum, whatever it may be, should be given, instead, to Judith."

"But the girl has no occasion for it," reasoned Mr. Hulet. "She will, as you say, have a moderate independence secured to her, but even then, I suppose, will continue to live under our roof?"

"No, uncle, she will not," answered Evy. "It was told me as a secret, but I think I am right in confiding to you, that Judith is engaged."

"That is very odd," said Mr. Hulet. "Sophia has often talked to me about the girl, and yet never mentioned that."

"It is the fact, nevertheless, for I had it from Judith's own lips, uncle. She is engaged to a young artist, whom Mrs. Mercer disapproves of on account of his poverty; and if the poor girl had a fortune of her own, there would be no obstacle to their happiness."

"Then, by gad! it shall be removed, if

I pay the money out of my own pocket," exclaimed Mr. Hulet. "Not that I am so very fond of Miss Judith myself, mark you; but for the exactly opposite reason. To tell you the truth, the notion of having that girl an inmate of my house for life somewhat appalled me. My hope was that that antipodean creature—what's his name?—Paragon, would be fool enough to marry her out of hand; but if she has already found a victim, so much the better. I don't mind buying the flowers for that sacrifice, at the cost of a few thousands. If Sophia declines to portion the young woman, I'll do it myself; so you may make your mind perfectly easy upon that score."

"A thousand thanks, dear uncle; it will be a great pleasure to me to tell Judith such good news. But you must promise not to breathe a word to my aunt about the young artist."

"I promise that, my dear, with all my

heart, and the more easily since I have nothing to breathe," replied Mr. Hulet, smiling; "you have not even mentioned his name. What is it?"

"Well, the fact is, I don't know what it is," said Evy, smiling in her turn. "She only calls him her Augustus."

"Ah! well I pity her Augustus, that's all—I may be about to do a foolish thing, myself," added Mr. Hulet, musingly; "I dare say I am; but Miss Judith's Augustus —however, you have taken the young woman under your protection, and therefore I will not say a word against her."

"But what have you to say against poor Judith, uncle?"

"Nothing, Evy, nothing. I don't like her, I confess; and yet I can't give you my reason for it:

"'I do not like thee, Doctor Fell,
The reason why I cannot tell,
But this I know, and know full well,
I do not like thee, Doctor Fell.'

By-the-by, talking of doctors, how I hate Doctor Carambole. However," here he sighed, "it's too late now to think of that—one more kiss, my darling Evy, and good-night."

CHAPTER XIV.

AN UNWILLING CONFIDENCE.

"RUMOUR, full of tongues," must necessarily have always had a good many stories to tell, but the older she gets, as it seems to me, the more garrulous she becomes. The institution of the telegraph and of the penny dailies, of course, awakens a thousand echoes more or less untrustworthy, as well as enlarges the sphere of her operations; but independently of them, scandal is more rife. The mention of that mysterious word—so dear to newspaper writers—"transpire," has had, I am inclined to believe, a baleful effect; and what we don't hear to the disadvantage of our fellow-creatures, we contrive to take in, like Joey Ladle, "through the pores."

Except upon some such supposition how is it to be accounted for that every tenant of Lucullus Mansion by ten A.M., on the morning after that fateful picnic, was not only in possession of the fact that Mr. Angelo Hulet was engaged to marry Mrs. Sophia Mercer, but that each had a totally different, and at the same time an entirely dependable account of the matter; a special and exclusive edition published gratuitously in confidential whispers. It was love at first sight; it was an old attachment; he had loved her hopelessly as somebody else's wife; she had loved him despairingly as somebody else's husband. There was no end in short to the various versions of the affair, and some of them reflected anything but credit upon the two respectable persons who were the objects of all this speculation. Such very queer questions, indeed, were asked of Evy by some of her own sex, couched in a tone of sympathy and condolence that made them fifty times more shocking, that she was at her wit's end what to answer. She had not received permission from her uncle to disclose the true state of the case, and she shrank from asking it of him, while Mrs. Mercer, in a private interview before breakfast, had laid on her a positive injunction of secrecy.

"Don't speak of it, my dear; I can scarcely bear to think of it. The idea of my having been your aunt these twenty years without your knowing it! I am delighted, of course; scarcely less on your account, my dear girl, than on my own. But don't let us speak of it; at all events just at present. Push me my footstool. Doctor Carambole says that to one in my critical state of health, emotion may be destruction. Pass me my drops."

But it was impossible to permit her respected relatives, who now paraded the garden side by side, or sat within doors with the arms of their arm-chairs almost interlaced, in defiance or ignorance of what anybody was saying about them, to be for many days under such shocking suspicions, and Evy took heart of grace and told Mrs. Hodlin Barmby all about it.

It was not easy to astonish, by any social revelation, the mistress of Lucullus Mansion, but this news did take that lady considerably aback.

"You surprise me, my dear Evy, beyond all expression," said she. "I could have staked my existence, for one thing, that your aunt, as she turns out to be, was an old maid. Of course, I took your uncle for a widower, and a very determined one. It is unaccountable to me that having once taken such a step as to separate from his wife, he should retract it. It is very creditable to our sex, my dear, is it not?"

"Indeed, Mrs. Barmby, I don't see that," said Evy, not without some indignation, for she had not reached that time of life when ladies desert their colours and go over to the other side, on such occasions. "I think it is only natural that my uncle's heart should soften toward the companion of his youth, and regret his estrangement from her. Ever since he met her, the remembrance of the past has affected him deeply, as I could well perceive, though, of course, I was ignorant of the cause."

"You don't say so! Well, now, I should have thought Mr. Hulet—kind, excellent gentleman as he is—would have been no more affected by old times, that is in a sentimental way, than by last week's newspaper. To be sure he seems very fond of her; in fact, to persons unaware of the peculiar circumstances of the case, rather demonstratively so. I conclude," added Mrs. Barmby, with some anxiety, "they are not going to remain with us very long."

"I rather think not," said Evy, simply. "My uncle, who finds himself much benefited by his sojourn at Balcombe, is going to take a house in the neighbourhood, I believe; my aunt and he, indeed, are gone together this very afternoon to look at Cliff Cottage."

"I saw them go," replied Mrs. Barmby, "and very much together they were. You were quite right to confide in me, my dear, quite; but people's tongues will wag in spite of the most satisfactory statements; and I fear it will be a little difficult to explain matters even now."

Mrs. Barmby's forebodings were amply realized. It had been noticed that Evy and herself were engaged in confidential conversation, and no sooner was their talk concluded than more than one lady made excuse for "interviewing" the mistress of the house, and sounding her upon the all-important topic. Such persons would have had to sink their artesian wells of inquiry very deep indeed in the case of Mrs. Hodlin Barmby, and perhaps not to find truth at the bottom of them after all, had that lady been minded to conceal it, but as it was she retailed to them what she had just heard. Mrs. Bullion, who rarely condescended to mingle with the rest, but remained for the most part in her apartments—engaged, it was rumoured, in financial operations upon her own account—was the last to hear the news, drops of which, however, had mysteriously permeated to her through the walls (which, as we know, have ears), and tempted her from her retirement.

"What is this I hear?" inquired she,

of Mrs. General Storks, who was not usually honoured with her notice, but who happened to be the first she met, "about Mr. Hulet aud Mrs. Mercer? Is it really true that they are engaged to one another?"

"I understand so, madam," replied the widow, gravely, "and also that they have taken Cliff Cottage."

"Taken the cottage! Why that seems a little precipitous, does it not?"

"The garden is so, very," answered Mrs. Stork. "I think it scarcely safe for one so near-sighted as Mrs. Mercer to walk in it."

"I was referring to the haste of their proceedings," explained Mrs. Bullion, majestically, "and not to the perpendicular nature of the locality. They are going to be married then, I conjecture, almost immediately?"

"No they're not," replied Mrs. Storks,

carelessly, and holding the lace-work on which she was engaged at a critical angle. "They are not going to be married at all."

Mrs. Bullion's full height was about five feet eight; she drew herself up to five feet nine; while her jaw fell almost an inch and a half, and with an audible click. If the Funds had dropped twenty per cent. she could scarcely have evinced greater horror.

"They are going to live at Cliff Cottage, and not going to be married at all," repeated she, in stupefied accents.

"Just so," said Mrs. Storks; "if you'll kindly step out of the light, because this work requires all one's eyesight, I'll tell you all about it. You must know they've been married already; half a century ago," &c.

And so, within a few hours, the love story of Angelo and Sophia became public property, and was commented upon from one end of Balcombe to another, and in all its aspects. To Judith, Evy had herself communicated the facts, though not more confidentially, or with greater detail, than she had used with Mrs. Barmby. There was something about Judith, though she viewed her with no such disfavour as did others of her sex, that did not invite her confidence, and upon this subject especially, which to Evy herself was upon her uncle's account a sacred one, she feared to excite her cynical mirth. Even as it was, Judith showed her scorn for the elderly pair, who flattered themselves that they would find in their December the warmth that had been denied to their July, and only when Evy went on to speak of what Mr. Hulet had promised at her request to do for Judith, did she drop her mocking tone. Then, indeed, she became all gratitude and humility; called Evy her "benefactress, whose kindness she should never, never forget," and manifested signs of deep emotion. This did not, however, prevent her from attending to business. She congratulated Evy that since Mr. Hulet was already her aunt's husband, there would be no occasion for his making a fresh will, so that her future fortune would be precisely what it had been before—an idea that had not occurred to her companion; and then proceeding to her own affairs besought Evy to persuade her uncle to put his promise to ensure her independence into effect at once.

"Such generous resolutions are only too apt to die out, and it is always best to strike while the iron is hot," said she. "I am afraid you think me mean and mercenary, dear Evy, for being so importunate; but, ah! you do not know how bitter the bread of dependence is; when you tell me of this blessed sufficiency in store for me, I cannot believe my tingling ears, and long to see it realized. Moreover," added she, with a faltering voice and a down-droop of her long eyelashes, "you must not forget that all this is not pure selfishness, dear Evy."

"Indeed, indeed, I do not, Judith," protested her companion, earnestly, "I am well aware you are thinking of another far more than yourself."

"Ah! then you yourself must know what it is to love," cried Judith, looking quickly up. "Noble as your nature is, Evy, I thought there must be some sympathy at work to move you to such generosity as you have shown to me. I trust I may one day behold the object of your love, and tell him how you have striven, and what you have wrought, for me for his sake."

It is usually the pride of a young girl to confide to one of her own sex and age the story of her love, and yet there was something within her that forbade Evy to open her heart to her companion.

"I am not so happy as you imagine, Judith," answered she, evasively, conscious that she was crimson from brow to chin, but speaking as calmly as she could; "nor even so happy as yourself."

"No, because I have a confidante—a friend in whom I trust, and in whom I have reposed all, Evy; while you, I see, have none. I do not reproach you, however, dear, nor need you fear my curiosity; your secret is as safe from me as it would have been with me, should you have thought proper to disclose it."

"Indeed, Judith, you do me wrong," answered Evy, whom Judith's rebuke affected the more keenly since she felt it was deserved. "What I meant to say was that you were more fortunate than I, since a remediable want—that of mere money—is the only bar to your happiness, while, in my case, there are other obstacles."

"Indeed?" answered Judith, sympathisingly. "Oh, would that it lay in my power, as it has been in yours, to remove them."

The tenderness of Judith's tone, and the touch on her arm which accompanied it from Judith's hand, were too much for Evy's gentle nature; and she straightway told all the history of her engagement with her beloved Jack, which, after all, it was an immense pleasure to her to do.

Upon that subject, from which her gentle thoughts were never long absent, her lips were sealed as regarded her uncle, and sympathy was what she yearned for. The treasure of love does not lie in a girl's heart, like gold in a miser's chest, to be gloated over in secret only: she delights to show her glittering wealth to others, and to be wished joy of its possession, as a poet enjoys reading his verse in a friend's ear. To recount where and how she had first met her love, to paint his looks and to describe his talk, is in some sort to realize once more the fond experience.

Judith listened with rapt attention to her companion's recital; her fine eyes sparkling, and her dusky cheeks aglow with excitement.

"Your tale is a romance indeed, dear Evy, and worth a score of commonplace love stories such as mine," cried she, admiringly. "And so you will be Lady Dirleton, one day, and live in a grand house, and set the fashions to a county."

"Indeed, Judith, I don't know that; though if so great a happiness as to marry him I love is vouchsafed to me, I suppose these things will follow, since I trust he will not be disinherited for my sake. All I care for, however, is Jack himself."

"Of course," answered Judith, musing; "and yet it must be a fine thing to have wealth and title, and to rule others—or at least it seems so to me who have neither, and who have always been compelled to obey. How charming you will look, Evy, with a coronet upon your brow——"

"And a sceptre in my right hand like the Queen of Spades," broke in Evy, laughing; "well, no; I am afraid, since I cannot pretend to the philosophy of my uncle, who stigmatizes all such things as baubles, that I shall be scarcely equal to the weight of such greatness."

"Ah! you are like the lady of the Burleigh ballad, are you, whose great position weighed her down," answered Judith, in so sharp a tone that it almost seemed contemptuous:—

> "'Faint she grew and ever fainter,
>   As she murmured, "Oh, that he
> Were once more that landscape-painter
>   That did win my heart from me."'"

"Nay, I do not say that," replied Evy, with a touch of pride. "I trust I have enough of my uncle's good sense about me not to be dismayed by the prospect of an accidental distinction. And I must say, Judith, considering the profession of the man you love, that your quotation is not very complimentary to him."

"That is true," answered Judith, softly. "I was only speaking generally, of course. Such ideas in a girl in my position are, without doubt, absurdly out of place; but I confess I should like Augustus to turn out to be a peer of the realm, and to wear, myself, a coronet by right of it."

"It would become you vastly well," said Eva, simply, and regarding her beautiful companion with undisguised admiration. "I am sure no one who saw you so attired would believe you to be in the enjoyment of an 'honour to which you were not born.' But, heigho!" added she, with a little sigh, "the thing is but little more likely to happen to myself than to you,

Judith. More than five months have to elapse before I am permitted to see him, even if I do see him; and our prospects may be no brighter then than they are now."

CHAPTER XV.

CLIFF COTTAGE.

CLIFF COTTAGE—a residence whose appellation had something in it of the pride that apes humility, being in fact not a cottage at all, but a villa of considerable size—was situated a quarter of a mile or so beyond the last outskirts of Balcombe, in rather a remarkable position. The red sandstone rocks, of which the coast line was composed, were in that spot perpendicular, and had arranged themselves in a double line; and on the plateau of turf that interposed between them the house was placed. At back and front of it, therefore, there was a precipice of red rock, the head of the one in the clouds, and the foot of the other in the sea. A more romantic situation could scarcely have been imagined, nor indeed a more beautiful one, for so much of the plateau as was not occupied by the house itself was made into garden ground, where under shelter from the upper cliff even the least hardy flowers throve and flourished. Sheer as this shelter was, its soft material was honey-combed by wind and weather into a thousand fantastic shapes, ranging from a deep-set monastic cell, to some weird likeness to lettering, such as that which showed itself on Belshazzar's wall. On the lower cliff a more powerful graver —Ocean—had hewn out echoing caverns, guarded by gigantic pillars, but nothing of this could be seen from "the cliff walk," as it was called, which ran round the garden, and only by a low stone wall was separated from the sheer abyss.

It was said that the sea was encroaching upon Red Rock Bay, as the place was named, and that this fence had every five years or so to be removed, and placed more inland; but though such a consideration might, as Mr. Hulet laughingly remarked, "have affected a newly-married couple of the usual age," Cliff Cottage was likely to last his time and that of Mrs. Sophia also; while as for the garden getting smaller every lustrum, it was probable that their power of taking walks in it would decrease at the same rate, or even quicker. He did not think it necessary to consult the interests of the two young ladies in the matter, since Judith was already engaged, and his opinion of his own sex, if not very high, was sufficiently so to give him confidence that Evy would (for his own happiness) only too soon find a lover, even if Lord Dirleton's "Jack" should play her false.

It was only natural for one of his age and opinions to attach no great importance to Jack's fidelity. He loved his niece as the apple of his eye, but he could not sympathize with her in her love for another, and especially such a one as Captain Heyton, an empty-headed young aristocrat (for so Mr. Hulet had summed him up in his own mind) with a taste for horseflesh that might too probably end in ruin.

Unsolicited by Evy, for he was a man who did not need to be reminded of a promise, one of Mr. Hulet's first acts on taking possession of his new home was to make provision for Judith. His wife, indeed, had herself proposed to do so, but he would not hear of that. "It is I who have rendered the girl unnecessary to you," he argued, "and therefore it is my place to provide for her for the present; while as to the future, supposing that I survive you, I shall give effect of course to every wish that you may express respecting her."

But though a considerable sum had thus been placed at Judith's immediate disposal, she evinced no wish to throw herself at once into the arms of her Augustus, but contented herself with writing him epistles doubtless of a most affectionate kind, which she always took to the post-office herself, as being too precious to be intrusted to a letter-bag. To Evy, she explained this conduct as being dictated by Augustus himself, "who is proud, dear fellow, as he is poor, and insists upon gaining a position for himself, as he feels he is on the road to do, before taking the hand which, thanks to you, has been so amply dowered." Evy thought this strange, conceiving that were she in Judith's place she would have found arguments to overcome such scruples, as perhaps being unable to imagine that what was her own should not ipso facto be Jack's, but she could not but applaud the delicacy of sentiment which such self-denial evidenced in the young painter, while her uncle (to whom, under the circumstances, she thought it right to disclose the matter) only shrugged his shoulders, and pronounced "Augustus" to be a much wiser fellow than he had taken him for.

Mr. Hulet, as we have seen, did not like Judith. Invalid old gentlemen—when their complaint is deafness—have sometimes, at unlucky moments, flashes of hearing, and when they are almost stone blind, see things at times that might escape even the keen-sighted; and Mr. Hulet being neither deaf nor blind, had all the morbidly acute perceptions of an invalid. A glance of scorn, a movement of impatience at some unguarded moment upon Judith's part, had probably prejudiced him against her. But at all events he was so prejudiced, and though he was far too much of a gentleman to make display of the fact to one under his own roof and protection, he could have heard the news of Judith's departure from Cliff Cottage with considerable resignation. The attitude of benefactor towards her in which she insisted upon placing him embarrassed him exceedingly; while the humility in which she always clothed herself in her relations with his wife annoyed him even more, since it had a bad effect upon that lady in fostering those airs and graces, which in years ago so irritated him, and which it seemed she had discarded only during the short period of his second wooing; but still he bore with Judith as being, after all, but an insignificant item of the sum of ills which his own folly had brought upon himself. For to confess the truth, his reunion with the wife of his youth he had found to be a mistake—not to say an unmitigated failure. An occasional argument, with a political opponent, is well enough, and promotes a healthy tone of mind; but a member of the Commune would not be welcome to an admirer of the British House of Lords as a tenant of the same dwelling-house, and vice versâ. Nay, it is even said that the smaller the points of difference the more fiercely are they apt to be discussed between persons so thrown together. And similarly, though nothing is more agreeable to a valetudinarian than to compare his ailments for a few hours with those of another cripple, two persons living under the same roof, both afflicted with "nerves," are apt to quarrel. There is egotism in all illness; and an egotist requires a clear space about him, and especially one not occupied by another ego. The claims of such persons upon the attention of their fellow-creatures are apt to clash, and their wants to interfere with one another. The effect of their second experience of married life soon showed itself in the couple in question; Mrs. Hulet, in addition to her many physical maladies, fell into a chronic state of "protest." She assumed a silent, but very demonstrative attitude of suffering under oppression, and left it in no sort of doubt either to himself or to others as to who was the oppressor. Once, and only once, she had expressed this sentiment in words; it was on an occasion when he had forbade her going on the cliff walk without a companion—a really dangerous place at any time for one so shaky and short-sighted as herself, and especially so since it was her caprice to frequent it after dusk.

"Angelo," said she, in the presence, too, of both the girls, a circumstance which did not make the statement less unpleasant, "you always were a tyrant, and you always will be!"

"No, my dear, I am no tyrant," was her

husband's quiet rejoinder; "but I frankly allow that of late months—I don't know how many, it seems years—I have showed myself very weak, and on one particular occasion, to be a most enormous fool." No epithet, indeed, was too gigantic for him to apply to that act of weakness which had caused him (to use his own words) once more to take to himself, for better or worse, a woman concerning whom he ought to have known there could have been no such alternative. A bachelor might marry without much prejudice to his judgment; a widower might do so, through a misunderstanding of the doctrine of chances, or a too sanguine confidence that he would have better luck next time; but that a man should take the same wife the second time—under the impression that she might have improved, like wine, with years—words, he said, failed him to express the profundity of contempt that he felt for such an idiot. It was not magnanimous in Mr. Hulet thus to speak, even if he could not help entertaining the sentiments described, and it did no good. Those who heard him retailed his words to others, and in due time they got round to his wife's ears, not, as may be imagined, to the improvement of their mutual position. She grew more "aggravating" every day, and her husband more sour and irritated. The weak points in his character—which was a generous one in the main—were brought out under this course of treatment with painful distinctness. Irresolute, or resolute only by fits, in matters of moment, he was obstinate to excess in trifles. For example, being very careless in his habits, he had on one occasion left a glass of colourless but most powerful medicine in the dining-room, which, had he not chanced to return at the precise moment, would have been swallowed by Evy in mistake for a glass of water. Of this circumstance Mrs. Hulet made the most, not hesitating to make use of her husband's affection for Evy, who herself would gladly have passed over the affair in silence, as a weapon against him. "If even love for his niece could not restrain him from such acts of selfish carelessness, what motive could be expected to have weight with him?" &c. In consequence of which rebuke it became Mr. Hulet's practice to leave his medicines about so recklessly, and in every room in the house, that a chance visitor to Cliff Cottage might well have been excused for taking it for a dispensary.

The cottage had many visitors, and habitual ones, including not only the neighbours, who were very friendly, but many of their old acquaintances at Lucullus Mansion, almost all of whom were fixtures there. Among these Mr. Paragon was one of the most constant "droppers in ;" he was seldom or never a guest, because Mr. Hulet disliked him, but for that very reason the mistress of the house encouraged his visits.

We have said that Judith's conduct towards her Augustus had seemed strange to Evy, but her behaviour to the Australian millionaire was a matter of much greater amazement. If, in fact, she had not known for certain that Judith's hand was engaged elsewhere, she would have thought it, if not the property of Mr. Paragon, at least to be had for the asking. It was no business of Evy's, of course, but this behaviour shocked her to that extent that she was driven to remonstrate with her young friend : a somewhat dangerous experiment, which, however, the other took in excellent part.

"There will be no hearts broken, my dear Evy, I promise you, however serious matters may appear. Mr. Paragon and I quite understand one another. And as for

Augustus, he has all the confidence in me which I have in myself. And that," added she, with a little laugh that grated on her friend's ear, " is very considerable."

Evy, though by no means satisfied with this reply, said no more on the subject, and the time was now drawing on towards an event which naturally monopolized her thoughts, to the exclusion of every other topic, namely, the April steeple-chases at Balcombe, for which, in the list of other gallant animals, she read in the local journal, with heartfelt joy, that Captain Heyton's Walltopper was entered.

END OF VOL. I.

www.ingramcontent.com/pod-product-compliance
Lightning Source LLC
Chambersburg PA
CBHW031328230426
43670CB00006B/280